The Ultimate Ninja Creami Cookbook for Beginners

Simple Innovative Ninja Creami Recipe Book | Indulge in Sweet Frozen Magic from Classic to Creative, Explore the World of Ninja Creami

Beverly McGraw

© Copyright 2024-All Rights Reserved.

This document is geared towards providing exact and reliable information concerning the topic and issue covered. The publication is sold with the idea that the publisher is not required to render accounting, officially permitted, or otherwise, qualified services. If advice is necessary, legal or professional, a practiced individual in the profession should be ordered.

In no way is it legal to reproduce, duplicate, or transmit any part of this document in either electronic means or in printed format. Recording of this publication is strictly prohibited, and any storage of this document is not allowed unless with written permission from the publisher. All rights reserved.

The information provided herein is stated to be truthful and consistent, in that any liability, in terms of inattention or otherwise, by any usage or abuse of any policies, processes, or Instructions: contained within is the solitary and utter responsibility of the recipient reader. Under no circumstances will any legal responsibility or blame be held against the publisher for any reparation, damages, or monetary loss due to the information herein, either directly or indirectly.

Respective authors own all copyrights not held by the publisher.

The information herein is offered for informational purposes solely and is universal as such. The presentation of the information is without a contract or any type of guarantee assurance.

The trademarks that are used are without any consent, and the publication of the trademark is without permission or backing by the trademark owner. All trademarks and brands within this book are for clarifying purposes only, are owned by the owners themselves, and are not affiliated with this document.

Contents

01	Introduction	
02	Fundamentals of Ninja Creami	
08	Chapter 1 Milkshakes	
18	Chapter 2 Smoothie Bowls	
28	Chapter 3 Ice Creams	
38	Chapter 4 Ice Creams Mix-Ins	
47	Chapter 5 Sorbets	
57	Chapter 6 Gelato	
66	Conclusion	
67	Appendix 1 Measurement Conversion Chart	
68	Appendix 2 Recipes Index	

Introduction

We all love ice creams, especially during the hot, sunny days. Many times, you will find people lining up in the ice cream shops to grab their favorite ice cream flavor. Their creamy, cool nature and, above all, the sweetness of ice creams make it hard to resist at any given time. However, did you know you can make your best ice cream and other nutritious recipes in the comfort of your home? All you need is a Ninja Creami kitchen appliance.

Yes, making ice creams, sorbets, milkshakes, smoothies, and other cool desserts can be hard at home, especially when you need freezer-type desserts for your family of guests coming over. But then, once you grab your Ninja Creami, the hassle will be all gone.

Anyone can afford a Ninja Creami, and with the simplified manual, anyone can operate the appliance. Therefore, don't deny yourself an opportunity to enjoy the best cool treaties when you can sort all your needs with this amazing kitchen appliance.

Coming from the Ninja Kitchen, one of the biggest kitchen appliances manufacturers, you are guaranteed great quality when it comes to this incredible kitchen device.

With a few tips, caring for and maintaining your Ninja Creami, along with other useful information, you will realize that this incredible kitchen equipment is worth your investment. Why wait any longer? Get your Ninja Creami and start trying out the many recipes detailed in this cookbook. You can also get extra creative and innovative in the kitchen and make varied flavors of different frozen treaties courtesy of the Ninja Creami.

Fundamentals of Ninja Creami

What is Ninja Creami?

The Ninja Creami is a sophisticated and powerful kitchen device that will simplify the processes of making ice cream and other freezer treaties right from your home. You won't need to buy ready-made cool treaties, whether you have a function or if you are making it for your family, thanks to the Ninja Creami kitchen equipment.

Features and Accessories

The Ninja Creami is a simplified kitchen appliance with simplified features that make ice cream preparation simple. The appliance comes with:

- Creamerizer Paddle
- Creami Pint Lid
- Outer Bowl
- Outer Bowl Lid
- 16 oz. Creami Pint
- Motor Base

The features include:

Appearance

The Ninja Creami is made with a simplified design, is highly portable, and is light in weight, making it one of the best kitchen appliances. It won't take up much space on your kitchen counter. It has a removable bowl that makes the cleaning process easier.

The ideal dimensions of the Ninja Creami are 11.8" by 4.5"

The Ninja Creami comes with the following functionalities and buttons that make work easier:

Install Light

This function will signal you if the assembling process isn't done appropriately. For instance, when blinking, it signals you that the bowl is not fitted properly, and you need to re-adjust it.

Progress Bar

Once you select the functionality you want on your Ninja Creami, this progress bar will show you the progress of the functionality going on.

One-click soft start

This feature enhances a delayed start. It enables the Ninja Creami to switch on gently without causing any shocks or unexpected noise. Therefore, when you plug it in, it will take some time before it can pick up.

Automatic shut-off timer

This feature enables the appliance to start counting down after 60 minutes. Therefore, if you have other commitments, you can meet other objectives as the machine is in operation without having to worry about shutting it off. It will shut off automatically once done. This is one unique feature that is not available on other similar appliances in the market!

Electronic weight display

One thing about making recipes is using the correct ingredient quantity. It can be hard to measure or estimate the required quantity, especially if the kitchen appliance you are using doesn't have a feature that simplifies this process. However, with Ninja Creami, the electronic weight display makes it possible for the user to weigh the ingredients as they add. This feature makes it possible to use the Ninja Creami for home production and for commercial production.

Freezer bowl

You can remove this freezer bowl at any moment and prepare any frozen dessert mix. With the freezer bowl removed, it is easy to move the appliance anywhere with ease.

Storage bags

These storage bags come in handy when you want to keep the bowl in the freezer when you aren't using it.

Cutting blade

Made with stainless steel material, the Ninja Creami comes with a cutting blade that enables you to shatter ice crystals meant to give the ice cream its creamy nature. Along the cutting blade are the agitator paddle and automated stirrer that simplifies the stirring process.

Multi-stage automated time

The automated time helps you get the best consistency of the treaties you are making. Be it a smoothie, ice cream, milkshake, or any other frozen dessert treat, you will always get the best results, thanks to the multi-stage automated timer feature.

The temperature control system

This functionality also plays a key role in ensuring you get the best results in terms of the consistency of the dessert you are making.

A transparent display screen

The powerful Ninja Creami has a transparent display screen where you can watch the timer and temperature settings. Besides, the top-notch display screen makes it possible to view the progress of your delicious treats.

In addition, here are the ingredients you may need to use the Ninja Creami.

Main ingredients used in Ninja Creami

One thing you will love about Ninja Creami is the fact that you have full control of all the ingredients used when preparing frozen desserts. This means that you can always adjust the ingredients to suit your preference, and if you have allergies to some ingredients, you can always adjust. However, make sure you have adequate knowledge when doing ingredient substitutes because the final results are what matters the most. In any case, we have provided as many recipes as possible. Therefore, you will always find something interesting for you and your family. Below are the key ingredients for Ninja Creami that are used in most frozen dessert treats.

1. Non-dairy milk

This is for lactose-intolerant people. Milk options such as macadamia nut milk, cashew milk, rice milk, hemp milk, oat milk, quinoa milk, or any other nut milk make the best-frozen treats. Besides, they are lightweight, and they won't give your recipes unwanted or funny tastes.

2. Dairy

Some dairy ingredients used in Ninja Creami recipes include yogurt, cream cheese, light cream, heavy whipping cream, whole milk, and skimmed milk. It all depends on the recipe you are preparing.

3. Chocolate and cocoa powder.

You can buy chocolate anywhere, and it can be in bars, wafers, chips, blocks, or powder. Chocolate syrup or chocolate milk is also recommended.

4. Eggs.

When making gelato and many ice cream recipes, eggs are quite crucial. Go for unbroken and spotless eggs for great results. In any case, always follow the recipe guidelines when using eggs. Otherwise, a slight misinterpretation might lead to poor results.

5. Sweeteners, but not general sugar.

Of course, you will need that sweet taste in your dessert treats. When using Ninja Creami, there is a wide range of sweeteners you can choose from, apart from the general sugar used in cooking. Sweeteners such as fruits (natural taste), coconut sugar, agave nectar, molasses, dates, and maple syrup are usually used in making sorbets and ice creams, giving them that desirable taste.

Note: Sugar plays a key role in bringing out the best ice cream. Therefore, check the components, quality of sugar, and expiry date.

Again, unless the recipe suggests otherwise, avoid using molasses or honey instead of granulated sugar when making ice creams.

In the case of chocolates, semisweet chocolates usually have around 50 – 60% cacao. Dark chocolate, on the other hand, has around 60-70% cacao. Milk chocolate has the least amount of cacao, while white chocolate doesn't have any solid chocolate.

6. Extracts, flavorings, & alcohol.

All alcohol treats cannot be frozen because alcohol affects the freezing point of the ingredients added. When you make ice cream with rum, it will have a smoother texture as compared to traditional ice cream. Flavorings and extracts have a significant impact on the final product, especially when making ice creams.

Benefits of Ninja Creami

If you are planning to get a Ninja Creami appliance and don't know if the move is worth your money, be sure you are on the right move. Below are some of the benefits you will get when using the Ninja Creami kitchen device:

It's multi-functional

Ideally, many perceive the Ninja Creami as an ultimate ice cream maker. Besides, when you view this appliance for the first time, you might perceive it as an ideal ice cream maker. But then, did you know you can make varied frozen treaties with your Ninja Creami? Yes! That's right, from smoothies, sorbets, milkshakes, gelato, and all forms of frozen desserts in the comfort of your home.

Easy to use

Even a beginner won't have a hard time using the Ninja Creami for the first time. The device is self-explanatory, with every accessory defining its role clearly just by looking at it. What's more, the Ninja Creami comes packed with a detailed manual showing you what you can do in case you feel you are missing some knowledge on operating the machine.

Easy to customize

Well, the Ninja Creami isn't restricted to specific ingredients. You only need to ensure the ingredients are friendly with the appliance and won't cause any damage. This, therefore, implies that you can customize and produce treaties, especially ice cream with your favorite flavors. Here, you can use the veggies and fruits you enjoy the most.

Advocates for healthy living

Well, among the incredible functionalities the Ninja Creami has is the lite ice cream. With this feature, even if you are on a diet, you can easily make low-carb and low-fat frozen treats and enjoy them from the comfort of your home!

Quick processing time

Once the freezing part is over, the Ninja Creami takes only a few

minutes to finalize the process. The frozen ice cream recipe is broken down by the Creami, which breaks up ice crystals to make the silkiest and creamiest frozen dessert treaties of all kinds.

You can make it ahead of time.

The Ninja Creami is an advanced and high-tech kitchen appliance. It comes packed with a storage area, making it possible for you to make varied ice cream flavors in advance and store them, waiting for processing time. When you are ready, you simply select the process functionality, and you are good to go.

A clear display screen

The Ninja Creami has a detailed display screen, showing you all the functionalities and where to press whenever you want to make a specific frozen dessert treat.

Easy to maintain and clean

It is so easy to clean and maintain a Ninja Creami. Besides, accessories, when removed, are dishwasher safe. You only need to ensure you arrange them in the upper compartment of the dishwasher. What's more, you can easily hand wash the accessories. You only need water and soap. For stubborn stains, you only need to soak the accessories in warm water for a few minutes before doing the cleaning process.

Before the First Use

Before we can explore the steps to follow when using Ninja Creami, consider the safety measures highlighted below:

Safety measures and guidelines to know when handling the Ninja Creami equipment:

Ideally, safety in the kitchen is one of the main things to consider when making different meals and when handling different kitchen appliances. Even though the Ninja Creami is made with high standards in regard to safety precautions and overall quality, you shouldn't ignore the following basic rules and safety precautions:

1. Even if you have read articles and books about Ninja Creami, don't skip reading through the manual and understanding the functionalities of different accessories. This is the number one point you should always consider.
2. Once you purchase the Ninja Creami, always wash it well and rinse it with clean water before you can use it. We shall explain how to clean the Ninja Creami well in the next sub-sections of this cookbook.
3. Again, check all the parts of the Ninja Creami as you inspect for any breakages or damaged parts. Do not use any part if it's broken or compromised. Instead, get the replacements from the manufacturers.
4. Take note of all the guidelines and warnings as described in the manual. Remember, a Ninja Creami is an electric appliance, and failure to follow basic warnings and guidelines can result in unwanted injuries and accidents.
5. Even though the Ninja Creami has an automated timer, make it a habit to always unplug it from the socket and switch it off the socket.
6. Don't use a damaged cord. Consider seeking repair services from the manufacturer. Again, avoid using electric extensions when using your Ninja Creami.
7. Avoid using the Ninja Creami for outdoor activities. Strictly use this appliance in the kitchen for your household needs.
8. Always keep the cord in position. It should not hang over the counter or the table.
9. As you set the Ninja Creami on your kitchen counter, ensure the surface is even and dry. Besides, the Ninja Creami shouldn't be near any heating kitchen equipment like microwaves, ovens, and stoves.
10. Pets and kids shouldn't come near the Ninja Creami.
11. Stick to accessories or parts meant for Ninja Creami alone. Avoid the idea of trying unrelated accessories on Ninja Creami. In any case, if any of the appliances get damaged, place another order from the manufacturer or dealers' outlet for ninja kitchenware products. Using unrelated accessories can damage the appliance or destroy its functionality.
12. This isn't a food processor or a blender. Therefore, don't attempt to crush or grind ingredients.
13. Always add liquid when processing dry ingredients
14. When at work, keep your clothing, hands, and hair off the Ninja Creami.
15. Don't add any hard ingredients or ice for processing
16. Avoid putting any utensils or hands in the container when using the Ninja Creami
17. Ensure all the accessories are well-fitted and in position before using the Ninja Creami.

Step-By-Step Using Ninja Creami

Using the Ninja Creami is not a hard process. Especially if you have read the manual and understood most of the basics, you won't have a hard time using this incredible kitchen device. If you have ever used an ice cream maker before, then you will find it simple. Still, if you have never operated any similar device before, don't worry; follow the steps below:

Step 1: Fit all the accessories as required

Of course, the first step is to assemble all the accessories in place. Remember, even if the appliance is new, you must remove the accessories, clean, dry them, and reassemble them in place. Otherwise, if you don't fit the other parts in position, the Ninja Creami might not function promptly.

Step 2: Plug on the power socket

Next, plug the cord on the power socket, then switch it on. Of course, make sure the cord isn't damaged in any case and it is dry to avoid electric shocks or related accidents in the kitchen.

Step 3: Switch on the power button

On the control panel, you will see the power button clearly displayed. Switch it on.

Step 4: Onto the Ninja Creami pint container, add the ingredients

Once the Ninja Creami is on, fill the ingredients, ensuring you don't cross the max fill mark located on the pint container.

Step 5: Freeze

If the recipe directions ask you to freeze, put the lid on and freeze as indicated in the recipe instructions.

Step 6: Set the container onto the Ninja Creami

Next, fit the pint container to the Ninja Creami, then seal it in place.

Step 7: Select the appropriate settings

Now, here is when you select the Ninja Creami functionality based on the recipe you are making or following. It can be gelato, smoothie, sorbet, or ice cream. Select the mix-in functionality when you have mix-on ingredients.

Step 8: Enjoy!

That is it. The processes are that simple. It is now time to enjoy the freshly prepared treat of your choice.

Different Functionalities of Ninja Creami

Milkshake

For all types of refreshing, freshly made, and nutritious milkshake recipes, use the Milkshake functionality on your Ninja Creami appliance.

How to use the milkshake functionality

- Start by mixing all the ingredients and putting them in the Ninja Creami pint container to freeze for up to 24 hours.
- Remove the pint lid and place the pint in the outer bowl of Ninja Creami.
- Put the creamerizer paddle into position and lock the lid.
- Select the Milkshake function on the Ninja Creami for processing
- If not well-processed, press the Re-Spin functionality for your desired consistency.
- Serve your milkshake.

Smoothie

Whether you are making vegetable smoothies, vegetable smoothies, frozen or fresh smoothies, you will need to use this functionality on your Ninja Creami appliance.

How to use the smoothie functionality

- Add your ingredients to the Ninja Creami pint container.
- Put on the lid and freeze for up to 24 hours.
- Once frozen, remove the lid and put the lid into the outer bowl.
- Put the creamerizer paddle into position and lock the lid.
- Select the Smoothie functionality on the Ninja Creami for processing.
- Once complete, detach the outer bowl and remove it from the Ninja Creami.
- Press the Re-Spin function if your smoothie isn't well-processed.
- Serve.

Ice Cream

Just like its name, the Ice Cream function will transform your ingredients into sweet, creamy, and nutritious ice cream. You can make any ice cream with this functionality.

- Add ingredients to the pint containers of the Ninja Creami. Snap the lid on the pint and freeze for 24 hours if needed.
- Remove the pint lid and place the pint in the outer bowl of Ninja Creami.
- Put the creamerizer paddle into position and lock the lid.
- Select the Ice Cream functionality on the Ninja Creami for processing.
- Once complete, unlock the outer bowl, releasing it from the Ninja Creami.
- If the ice cream is not soft and smooth, select the re-spin functionality to get your desired consistency.
- Once done, serve the ice cream in bowls.

Lite Ice Cream

One thing about Ninja Creami is the fact that it has an option for those who are on a diet or prefer ice creams with low sugar and fat content. The Lite Ice Cream functionality will enable you to prepare healthy ice creams with low fat and sugar content.

Note: This function works similarly to the Ice Cream functionality. You only need to press the option "Lite ice Cream" instead of the "Ice Cream Functionality."

Sorbet

You will make creamy sorbets for a cool dessert treaty with the Sorbet functionality.

How to use the sorbet functionality

- Start by mixing the ingredients, then put them into the Ninja Creami pint container. Snap the lid on the pint and freeze for 24 hours if needed.
- Remove the pint lid and place the pint in the outer bowl of Ninja Creami.
- Put the creamerizer paddle into position and lock the lid.
- Select the Sorbet function on the Ninja Creami for processing.
- Once done, check the consistency.

- If not well-processed, select the Re-Spin function for creamer and soft results.
- Spoon into bowls and serve.
- Freeze any leftovers in air-tight containers.

Gelato

For all your Italian-style ice creams, the Gelato functionality has you covered.

How to use the gelato functionality

- Add ingredients to the pint containers of the Ninja Creami. Snap the lid on the pint and freeze for 24 hours.
- Remove the pint lid and put the pint in the outer bowl of the Ninja Creami.
- Put the creamerizer paddle into position and lock the lid.
- Select the Gelato functionality on the Ninja Creami for processing.
- Once complete, detach the outer bowl from the unit, then serve the gelato right away.

Mix-in

Of course, you might need to elevate and adjust your frozen dessert treats when preparing with your Ninja Creami. You might need to add nuts, crushed cookies, candy, pieces, or any other ingredient that will adjust the taste and flavor. In this case, use the Mix-in functionality.

How to use the mix-in functionality

For all your mix-in treaties, use the following steps:
- Mix the main ingredients, omitting the mix-ins.
- Add the mixed ingredients into the pint container of the Ninja Creami to freeze for up to 24 hours.
- Select the Ice Cream functionality to process.
- Once complete, add the mix-ins and select the mix-in functionality to process.
- Select Re-Spin for a creamier and softer consistency

Re-Spin

Your final mixture ought to be creamy and smooth. That is why the appliance is called Ninja "Creami". However, sometimes, the results can be crumbly and rough. In such a case, press the Re-Spin functionality.

Note: Do not use the re-spin functionality before using the mix-in functionality.

Tips for Using Ninja Creami

When using the Ninja Creami, the following tips will always come in handy, ensuring you get the most out of this incredible kitchen appliance.

Tips for freezing

Before you process the ingredients for freezing, use the following tips:
- Ensure you freeze the mixture for 24 hours and beyond
- The freezing temperature should be accurate. The recommended range for a Ninja Creami is between 90F and 70F.
- Avid processing ingredients that have not been fully frozen
- The pint should be on the appropriate level. Avoid freezing at an angle.
- When the mixture has frozen evenly, take off the lid and set the pint over the outer bowl of the machine.
- For mixtures that have frozen unevenly, remove the outer surface, then freeze again. Ideally, you can put it in the fridge before freezing once again.
- If possible, avoid chest freezers when using Ninja Creami because of the extremely cold temperatures. Therefore, upright freezers are the best for mixtures to be processed using a Ninja Creami.

Tips for mixing in

- Remember the following tips for the case of mix-in:
- Avoid the mix-in functionality for milkshake settings
- Avoid using sauces and spreads when making gelato and ice cream
- Chop or cube the ingredients into smaller bits when you want them in your ice cream
- Use ¼ cup of your preferred ingredients. It can be frozen fruits, chocolate pieces or shavings, seeds, nuts, crushed candies, and crushed cookies, among many others.
- Cookies and cereals are among the soft mix-ins. Therefore, they will remain minute once you use the mix-in functionality.

Cleaning and Caring for Ninja Creami

Once you acquire your Ninja Creami, that is not all. You should plan and learn how to care for and maintain the appliance to serve you better and last longer. Besides, when you take care and maintain the Ninja Creami appropriately, it guarantees proper preparation of the frozen dessert treaties, thus promoting healthy living.

1. How to clean the Ninja Creami

- Before you begin the process of cleaning your Ninja Creami, start by unplugging the appliance and then removing the Creamerizer paddle.

- In warm, soapy water, clean the container, paddles, and lids using a soft sponge.
- Rinse the cleaned parts in clean water, then put the accessories in a safe space to dry out well.
- Since the containers, lids, and paddles are dishwasher safe, make sure to situate them on the upper rack only during the cleaning process.
- For parts with stubborn and hard-to-remove stains, immerse them in warm and soapy water first for some minutes before washing. This will make the cleaning process simple and save you more time.
- Use a dry, clean kitchen cloth to wipe the outer parts of the Ninja Creami

Note: Avoid using brushes or abrasive pads when cleaning the motor base. This could cause some damage.

2. How to store Ninja Creami

When not in use after cleaning and drying, you should store the Ninja Creami in a manner that won't pose any harm to the appliance or people around. Therefore, follow the steps below to store your appliance appropriately:
- Fix the cord using the fastener located near the back part of the motor base
- Keep the Ninja Creami away from heat-generating kitchen appliances
- Also, store the device in a place kids can't reach.

3. How to reset the motor

The Ninja Creami is designed in a manner that it can stop functioning temporarily. This happens mostly when there are overloading cases. This feature helps to prevent the drive system and the motor from being damaged completely in case it is overloaded, hence the need for resetting. Therefore, when this happens, follow the steps below to reset your Ninja Creami:
- Remove the device from the plug.
- Give it approximately 15 – 30 minutes to cool
- Extract the outer bowl lid and the paddle
- Confirm if any ingredients are stuck on the lid; remove if any.
- Reassemble the unit.

4. How to ensure you don't overload the Ninja Creami

1. Stick to the maximum capacity mark. There is always a clear line showing the maximum number of ingredients the container can hold. Don't pass this mark, lest you overload the Ninja Creami, making it fail to operate promptly.
2. Avoid filling solid ice cubes or blocks in your Ninja Creami
3. Don't use ingredients that are hard to lose, especially big chunks of frozen fruits. In any case, try to thaw the fruit chunks first before adding them to the Ninja Creami. Still, you can cube or slice them into smaller pieces.

Frequently Asked Questions & Notes

1. Why won't my Ninja Creami appliance turn on?

There are some basic reasons that can make your appliance fail to function appropriately. Start by checking if all the accessories are well-fitted. You can opt to detach the accessories and then reassemble them. Another possible cause that can make your Ninja Creami fail to function is the automatic shut-off feature as a result of overloading it. In this case, you will need to restart your appliance to make it work again. Finally, check the power cord. It should be well-plugged in and switched on.

2. Why does my ice cream come out dry and crumbly after processing it?

There are several reasons that can make your ice cream turn out dry and crumbly. For instance, extremely low-temperature settings at the base. In this case, you only need to detach the device, reassemble it, and then select the re-spin functionality. This will increase the processing time, thus producing a smooth ice cream texture.

Another possible reason for a crumbly and dry ice cream is low fat and sugar content. In this case, use the guidelines given in each recipe for best results.

3. Can I use other accessories from other brands in my Ninja Creami?

No. You shouldn't attempt to use other parts in your newly acquired Ninja Creami. In case of the accessories get damaged, it is recommended that you seek a replacement from the Ninja Creami manufacturers. Remember, the Ninja Creami accessories are specifically made to fit in the appliance without any compromise.

4. How many servings can I get when using the Ninja Creami?

The Ninja Creami comes packed in containers with a capacity of 1 pint. The total number of containers is three. The best part is that you can always buy some more containers from the nearby stores and produce more treats. You only need to ensure you purchase containers meant for the Ninja Creami.

Chapter 1 Milkshakes

Tasty Peanut Butter Strawberry Milkshake	09
Lemony Pineapple Sherbet Milkshake	09
Rich Mango Milkshake..	10
Easy Strawberry Milkshake...	10
Sweet Vanilla Pistachio Milkshake	11
Vanilla Avocado Milkshake	11
Chocolate Chip Cookie Milkshake	12
Vanilla Blueberry Milkshake	12
Oreo Chocolate Milkshake	13
Mango Cinnamon Milkshake with Walnuts	13
Peanut Butter Chocolate Milkshake	14
Delicious Coffee Coconut Milkshake	14
Boozy Chocolate Milkshake	15
Vanilla Banana Milkshake	15
Creamy Strawberry Milkshake	16
Simple Pistachio Ice Cream Milkshake	16
Fresh Pineapple Milkshake	17
Banana Coffee Milkshake...	17

Tasty Peanut Butter Strawberry Milkshake

⏰ **Prep: 10 minutes** 🍰 **Serves: 2**

Ingredients:

1½ cups strawberry ice cream
½ cup unsweetened almond milk
¼ cup peanut butter
¼ teaspoon vanilla extract

Preparation:

1. In an empty Ninja CREAMi pint container, put in ice cream. 2. Top with the remaining ingredients and lightly blend to incorporate. 3. Arrange the container into the outer bowl of Ninja CREAMi. 4. Install the "Creamerizer Paddle" onto the lid of outer bowl. 5. Then rotate the lid clockwise to lock. 6. Press "Power" button to turn on the unit. 7. Then press "MILKSHAKE" button. 8. When the program is completed, turn the outer bowl and release it from the machine. 9. Transfer the shake into serving glasses and enjoy immediately.

Serving Suggestions: Serve with a topping of whipped cream.
Variation Tip: You can use milk of your choice.
Nutritional Information per Serving: Calories: 300 |Fat: 22.1g|Sat Fat: 6.7g|Carbohydrates: 17.9g|Fiber: 2.4g|Sugar: 13.9g|Protein: 11g

Lemony Pineapple Sherbet Milkshake

⏰ **Prep: 10 minutes** 🍰 **Serves: 2**

Ingredients:

1½ cups pineapple sherbet
½ cup lemon seltzer

Preparation:

1. In an empty Ninja CREAMi pint container, put sherbet and top with lime seltzer. 2. Arrange the container into the outer bowl of Ninja CREAMi. 3. Install the "Creamerizer Paddle" onto the lid of outer bowl. 4. Then rotate the lid clockwise to lock. 5. Press "Power" button to turn on the unit. 6. Then press "MILKSHAKE" button. 7. When the program is completed, turn the outer bowl and release it from the machine. 8. Transfer the shake into a serving glasses and enjoy immediately.

Serving Suggestions: Serve with a garnishing of maraschino cherry.
Variation Tip: You can use lemon-lime soda instead of lemon seltzer.
Nutritional Information per Serving: Calories: 190 |Fat: 2.1g|Sat Fat: 1.9g|Carbohydrates: 39.5g|Fiber: 0.8g|Sugar: 29g|Protein: 1.6g

Rich Mango Milkshake

⏰ **Prep: 10 minutes**   ≋ **Serves: 2**

Ingredients:

1½ cups mango ice cream
¼ cup mango, peeled, pitted and sliced
½ cup whole milk

Preparation:

1. In an empty Ninja CREAMi pint container, put the ice cream. 2. Top with the mango slices and milk and gently blend to incorporate. 3. Arrange the container into the outer bowl of Ninja CREAMi. 4. Install the "Creamerizer Paddle" onto the lid of outer bowl. 5. Then rotate the lid clockwise to lock. 6. Press "Power" button to turn on the unit. 7. Then press "MILKSHAKE" button. 8. When the program is completed, turn the outer bowl and release it from the machine. 9. Transfer the shake into serving glasses and enjoy immediately.
Serving Suggestions: Serve with a garnishing of pistachios.
Variation Tip: Use fresh mango chunks.
Nutritional Information per Serving: Calories: 163 | Fat: 6.7g|Sat Fat: 4.1g|Carbohydrates: 22.3g|Fiber: 2.6g|Sugar: 16.8g|Protein: 4.1g

Easy Strawberry Milkshake

⏰ **Prep: 10 minutes**   ≋ **Serves: 2**

Ingredients:

1½ cups strawberry ice cream
½ cup whole milk
½ cup fresh strawberries, hulled and cut up

Preparation:

1. In an empty Ninja CREAMi pint container, put in ice cream, followed by milk and strawberry pieces. 2. Arrange the container into the outer bowl of Ninja CREAMi. 3. Install the "Creamerizer Paddle" onto the lid of outer bowl. 4. Then rotate the lid clockwise to lock. 5. Press "Power" button to turn on the unit. 6. Then press "MILKSHAKE" button. 7. When the program is completed, turn the outer bowl and release it from the machine. 8. Transfer the shake into serving glasses and serve immediately.
Serving Suggestions: Serve with a garnishing of fresh strawberries.
Variation Tip: You can use milk of your choice.
Nutritional Information per Serving: Calories: 154 | Fat: 6.7g|Sat Fat: 4g|Carbohydrates: 18.3g|Fiber: 1.1g|Sugar: 14.8g|Protein: 3.8g

Sweet Vanilla Pistachio Milkshake

⏱ Prep: 10 minutes   ▧ Serves: 2

▸ **Ingredients:**

1½ cups vanilla ice cream
½ cup whole milk
2 tablespoons maple syrup
¼ cup pistachios, chopped
¼ teaspoon vanilla extract

▸ **Preparation:**

1. In an empty Ninja CREAMi pint container, put ice cream, followed by milk, maple syrup, pistachios and vanilla extract. 2. Arrange the container into the outer bowl of Ninja CREAMi. 3. Install the "Creamerizer Paddle" onto the lid of outer bowl. 4. Then rotate the lid clockwise to lock. 5. Press "Power" button to turn on the unit. 6. Then press "MILKSHAKE" button. 7. When the program is completed, turn the outer bowl and release it from the machine. 8. Transfer the shake into serving glasses and enjoy immediately.

Serving Suggestions: Serve with a garnishing of extra pistachios.
Variation Tip: You can use milk of your choice.
Nutritional Information per Serving: Calories: 254 |Fat: 13.1g|Sat Fat: 4.9g|Carbohydrates: 32.8g|Fiber: 2.9g|Sugar: 29g|Protein: 4.9g

Vanilla Avocado Milkshake

⏱ Prep: 10 minutes   ▧ Serves: 2

▸ **Ingredients:**

1 cup vanilla ice cream
1 small ripe avocado, peeled, pitted and chopped
1 teaspoon fresh lime juice
2 tablespoons honey
1 teaspoon vanilla extract
½ cup whole milk

▸ **Preparation:**

1. In an empty Ninja CREAMi pint container, put ice cream, followed by remaining ingredients. 2. Arrange the container into the outer bowl of Ninja CREAMi. 3. Install the "Creamerizer Paddle" onto the lid of outer bowl. 4. Then rotate the lid clockwise to lock. 5. Press "Power" button to turn on the unit. 6. Then press "MILKSHAKE" button. 7. When the program is completed, turn the outer bowl and release it from the machine. 8. Transfer the shake into serving glasses and enjoy immediately.

Serving Suggestions: Serve with a garnishing of banana slices.
Variation Tip: You can use sweetener of your choice.
Nutritional Information per Serving: Calories: 373 |Fat: 23.7g|Sat Fat: 6.4g|Carbohydrates: 39g|Fiber: 8.5g|Sugar: 27.6g|Protein: 4.1g

Chocolate Chip Cookie Milkshake

⏰ **Prep: 10 minutes**   ⬙ **Serves: 2**

Ingredients:

1 cup whole milk
½ cup chocolate creamer
¼ cup chocolate liqueur
1 tablespoon honey
¼ teaspoon vanilla extract
¼ cup chocolate chip cookies, chopped

Preparation:

1. In an empty Ninja CREAMi pint container, put milk and remaining ingredients except for cookies and blend to incorporate. 2. Cover the container with the storage lid and freeze for 24 hours. 3. After 24 hours, take off the lid from container and arrange into the outer bowl of Ninja CREAMi. 4. Install the "Creamerizer Paddle" onto the lid of outer bowl. 5. Then rotate the lid clockwise to lock. 6. Press "Power" button to turn on the unit. 7. Then press "MILKSHAKE" button. 8. When the program is completed, turn the outer bowl and release it from the machine. 9. Transfer the shake into serving glasses, top with chocolate chip cookies, and enjoy immediately.

Serving Suggestions: Serve with a topping of whipped cream.
Variation Tip: You can use maple syrup instead of honey.
Nutritional Information per Serving: Calories: 375 |Fat: 18.6g|Sat Fat: 9.9g|Carbohydrates: 26.1g|Fiber: 1.6g|Sugar: 42.9g|Protein: 6.8g

Vanilla Blueberry Milkshake

⏰ **Prep: 10 minutes**   ⬙ **Serves: 2**

Ingredients:

1½ cups blueberry ice cream
½ cup whole milk
¼ teaspoon vanilla extract

Preparation:

1. In an empty Ninja CREAMi pint container, put in ice cream, followed by milk and vanilla extract. 2. Arrange the container into the outer bowl of Ninja CREAMi. 3. Install the "Creamerizer Paddle" onto the lid of outer bowl. 4. Then rotate the lid clockwise to lock. 5. Press "Power" button to turn on the unit. 6. Then press "MILKSHAKE" button. 7. When the program is completed, turn the outer bowl and release it from the machine. 8. Transfer the shake into serving glasses and enjoy immediately.

Serving Suggestions: Serve with a topping of crushed cookies.
Variation Tip: Whole milk can be replaced with non-dairy milk.
Nutritional Information per Serving: Calories: 141 |Fat: 7.2g|Sat Fat: 4.5g|Carbohydrates: 14.8g|Fiber: 0.4g|Sugar: 13.8g|Protein: 3.7g

Oreo Chocolate Milkshake

⏰ **Prep: 10 minutes** 📚 **Serves: 2**

Ingredients:

1½ cups chocolate ice cream
3-4 Oreo cookies, crushed
¼ cup coconut milk

Preparation:

1. In an empty Ninja CREAMi pint container, put in ice cream. 2. With a spoon, create a 1½-inch wide hole in the center that reaches the bottom of the pint container. Add the cookies into the hole and top with milk. 3. Arrange the container into the outer bowl of Ninja CREAMi. 4. Install the "Creamerizer Paddle" onto the lid of outer bowl. 5. Then rotate the lid clockwise to lock. 6. Press "Power" button to turn on the unit. 7. Then press "MILKSHAKE" button. 8. When the program is completed, turn the outer bowl and release it from the machine. 9. Transfer the shake into a serving glass and enjoy immediately.

Serving Suggestions: Serve with a topping of extra cookies.
Variation Tip: Use full-fat coconut milk.
Nutritional Information per Serving: Calories: 242 |Fat: 15.3g|Sat Fat: 10.3g|Carbohydrates: 24.4g|Fiber: 1.5g|Sugar: 17.6g|Protein: 3.2g

Mango Cinnamon Milkshake with Walnuts

⏰ **Prep: 10 minutes** 📚 **Serves: 2**

Ingredients:

1½ cups mango ice cream
½ cup whole milk
2 tablespoons maple syrup
¼ cup walnuts, cut up
½ teaspoon ground cinnamon

Preparation:

1. In an empty Ninja CREAMi pint container, put in ice cream, followed by milk, maple syrup, walnuts and cinnamon. 2. Arrange the container into the outer bowl of Ninja CREAMi. 3. Install the "Creamerizer Paddle" onto the lid of outer bowl. 4. Then rotate the lid clockwise to lock. 5. Press "Power" button to turn on the unit. 6. Then press "MILKSHAKE" button. 7. When the program is completed, turn the outer bowl and release it from the machine. 8. Transfer the shake into serving glasses and enjoy immediately.

Serving Suggestions: Serve with a topping of extra nuts.
Variation Tip: You can use nuts of your choice.
Nutritional Information per Serving: Calories: 290 |Fat: 16.5g|Sat Fat: 5.1g|Carbohydrates: 30.2g|Fiber: 1.8g|Sugar: 25.8g|Protein: 7.5g

Peanut Butter Chocolate Milkshake

⏰ **Prep: 10 minutes** ⚏ **Serves: 2**

Ingredients:

1½ cups chocolate ice cream
½ cup unsweetened chocolate almond milk
¼ cup peanut butter
¼ teaspoon vanilla extract

Preparation:

1. In an empty Ninja CREAMi pint container, put in ice cream. 2. Top with the remaining ingredients and lightly blend to incorporate. 3. Arrange the container into the outer bowl of Ninja CREAMi. 4. Install the "Creamerizer Paddle" onto the lid of outer bowl. 5. Then rotate the lid clockwise to lock. 6. Press "Power" button to turn on the unit. 7. Then press "MILKSHAKE" button. 8. When the program is completed, turn the outer bowl and release it from the machine. 9. Transfer the shake into serving glasses and enjoy immediately.
Serving Suggestions: Serve with a garnishing of maraschino cherry.
Variation Tip: You can use milk of your choice.
Nutritional Information per Serving: Calories: 304 |Fat: 22.4g|Sat Fat: 6.9g|Carbohydrates: 18.9g|Fiber: 2.6g|Sugar: 13.6g|Protein: 10g

Delicious Coffee Coconut Milkshake

⏰ **Prep: 10 minutes** ⚏ **Serves: 2**

Ingredients:

2 cups coffee ice cream
⅓ cup coffee liqueur
⅓ cup full-fat coconut milk
2-3 drops liquid stevia

Preparation:

1. In an empty Ninja CREAMi pint container, put in ice cream, followed by chocolate liqueur and milk. 2. Arrange the container into the outer bowl of Ninja CREAMi. 3. Install the "Creamerizer Paddle" onto the lid of outer bowl. 4. Then rotate the lid clockwise to lock. 5. Press "Power" button to turn on the unit. 6. Then press "MILKSHAKE" button. 7. When the program is completed, turn the outer bowl and release it from the machine. 8. Transfer the shake into serving glasses and enjoy immediately.
Serving Suggestions: Serve with a topping of whipped cream.
Variation Tip: Feel free to use sweetener of your choice.
Nutritional Information per Serving: Calories: 368 |Fat: 15.1g|Sat Fat: 11.9g|Carbohydrates: 39.1g|Fiber: 0.5g|Sugar: 36.2g|Protein: 3g

Boozy Chocolate Milkshake

⏱ Prep: 10 minutes   ◆ Serves: 2

> Ingredients:

- 2 cups chocolate creamer
- 1 tablespoon honey
- 2 ounces vodka
- 1 tablespoon cacao nibs

> Preparation:

1. In an empty Ninja CREAMi pint container, put creamer, honey and vodka and blend to incorporate thoroughly. 2. Cover the container with storage lid and freeze for 24 hours. 3. After 24 hours, take off the lid from container and arrange into the outer bowl of Ninja CREAMi. 4. Install the "Creamerizer Paddle" onto the lid of outer bowl. 5. Then rotate the lid clockwise to lock. 6. Press "Power" button to turn on the unit. 7. Then press "MILKSHAKE" button. 8. When the program is completed, turn the outer bowl and release it from the machine. 9. Transfer the shake into serving glasses and serve immediately.

Serving Suggestions: Serve with the topping of chocolate shavings.
Variation Tip: For more flavor, use vanilla vodka.
Nutritional Information per Serving: Calories: 559| Fat: 47.3g|Sat Fat: 29.1g|Carbohydrates: 17.5g|Fiber: 0.9g|Sugar: 8.1g|Protein: 6.6g

Vanilla Banana Milkshake

⏱ Prep: 10 minutes   ◆ Serves: 2

> Ingredients:

- 1 cup coconut ice cream
- 2 bananas, peel removed and sliced
- 1 tablespoon honey
- 1 teaspoon vanilla extract
- ½ cup whole milk

> Preparation:

1. In an empty Ninja CREAMi pint container, put in ice cream, followed by remaining ingredients. 2. Arrange the container into the outer bowl of Ninja CREAMi. 3. Install the "Creamerizer Paddle" onto the lid of outer bowl. 4. Then rotate the lid clockwise to lock. 5. Press "Power" button to turn on the unit. 6. Then press "MILKSHAKE" button. 7. When the program is completed, turn the outer bowl and release it from the machine. 8. Transfer the shake into serving glasses and enjoy immediately.

Serving Suggestions: Serve with a sprinkling of cinnamon.
Variation Tip: Honey can be replaced with maple syrup.
Nutritional Information per Serving: Calories: 248 |Fat: 5.9g|Sat Fat: 3.5g|Carbohydrates: 46.6g|Fiber: 3.3g|Sugar: 33.5g|Protein: 4.4g

Creamy Strawberry Milkshake

⏰ Prep: 10 minutes   ≋ Serves: 2

Ingredients:

2 cups strawberry ice cream
2 tablespoons cream liqueur
2 tablespoons vodka
½ teaspoon vanilla extract

Preparation:

1. In an empty Ninja CREAMi pint container, put in ice cream, followed by cream liqueur, vodka and vanilla extract. 2. Arrange the container into the outer bowl of Ninja CREAMi. 3. Install the "Creamerizer Paddle" onto the lid of outer bowl. 4. Then rotate the lid clockwise to lock. 5. Press "Power" button to turn on the unit. 6. Then press "MILKSHAKE" button. 7. When the program is completed, turn the outer bowl and release it from the machine. 8. Transfer the shake into serving glasses and enjoy immediately.
Serving Suggestions: Serve with a garnishing of fresh strawberries.
Variation Tip: Vodka can be replaced with rum.
Nutritional Information per Serving: Calories: 336 |Fat: 13.5g|Sat Fat: 8.5g|Carbohydrates: 28.6g|Fiber: 0.5g|Sugar: 24.1g|Protein: 3.8g

Simple Pistachio Ice Cream Milkshake

⏰ Prep: 10 minutes   ≋ Serves: 2

Ingredients:

2 cups pistachio ice cream
1 cup whole milk
¼ teaspoon vanilla extract
¼ teaspoon almond extract

Preparation:

1. In an empty Ninja CREAMi pint container, put in ice cream. 2. Top with the milk and both extracts and lightly blend to incorporate. 3. Arrange the container into the outer bowl of Ninja CREAMi. 4. Install the "Creamerizer Paddle" onto the lid of outer bowl. 5. Then rotate the lid clockwise to lock. 6. Press "Power" button to turn on the unit. 7. Then press "MILKSHAKE" button. 8. When the program is completed, turn the outer bowl and release it from the machine. 9. Transfer the shake into serving glasses and enjoy immediately.
Serving Suggestions: Serve with a topping of pistachios.
Variation Tip: You can use extract of your choice.
Nutritional Information per Serving: Calories: 212 |Fat: 11g|Sat Fat: 6.8g|Carbohydrates: 21.6g|Fiber: 0.5g|Sugar: 20.5g|Protein: 6.2g

Fresh Pineapple Milkshake

⏰ **Prep: 10 minutes**   ◆ **Serves: 2**

Ingredients:

1½ cups coconut ice cream
½ cup coconut milk
½ cup fresh pineapple, peel removed and cut up

Preparation:

1. In an empty Ninja CREAMi pint container, put in ice cream, followed by milk and pineapple pieces. 2. Arrange the container into the outer bowl of Ninja CREAMi. 3. Install the "Creamerizer Paddle" onto the lid of outer bowl. 4. Then rotate the lid clockwise to lock. 5. Press "Power" button to turn on the unit. 6. Then press "MILKSHAKE" button. 7. When the program is completed, turn the outer bowl and release it from the machine. 8. Transfer the shake into serving glasses and serve immediately.

Serving Suggestions: Serve with a garnishing of cherries.
Variation Tip: You can use vanilla ice cream instead of coconut ice cream.
Nutritional Information per Serving: Calories: 261 |Fat: 19.6g|Sat Fat: 16.1g|Carbohydrates: 20.7g|Fiber: 2.3g|Sugar: 16.6g|Protein: 3.3g

Banana Coffee Milkshake

⏰ **Prep: 10 minutes**   ◆ **Serves: 2**

Ingredients:

1½ cups vanilla ice cream
½ cup whole milk
½ cup banana, peel removed and cut into ½-inch pieces
1 tablespoon instant coffee powder
½ teaspoon vanilla extract

Preparation:

1. In an empty Ninja CREAMi pint container, put in ice cream, followed by milk, banana, coffee powder and vanilla extract. 2. Arrange the container into the outer bowl of Ninja CREAMi. 3. Install the "Creamerizer Paddle" onto the lid of outer bowl. 4. Then rotate the lid clockwise to lock. 5. Press "Power" button to turn on the unit. 6. Then press "MILKSHAKE" button. 7. When the program is completed, turn the outer bowl and release it from the machine. 8. Transfer the shake into serving glasses and serve immediately.

Serving Suggestions: Serve with a garnishing of banana slices.
Variation Tip: Use a ripe banana.
Nutritional Information per Serving: Calories: 176 |Fat: 7.4g|Sat Fat: 4.6g|Carbohydrates: 23.5g|Fiber: 1.4g|Sugar: 18.4g|Protein: 4.1g

Chapter 2 Smoothie Bowls

Creamy Banana Rum Smoothie Bowl 19

Papaya and Banana Smoothie Bowl 19

Honey Oats Tofu Smoothie Bowl 20

Nutritious Avocado Banana Smoothie Bowl 20

Tropical Mango Pineapple Smoothie Bowl 21

Banana Berry Smoothie Bowl 21

Citrus Blueberry Smoothie Bowl 22

Easy Peach Smoothie Bowl 22

Mango Banana Smoothie Bowl 23

Sweet Potato and Banana Smoothie Bowl 23

Delicious Chocolate Banana Smoothie Bowl 24

Honeyed Strawberry-Banana Smoothie Bowl 24

Chia Banana Smoothie Bowl 25

Orange Peach Smoothie Bowl 25

Tropical Yogurt Smoothie Bowl 26

Quick Raspberry Yogurt Smoothie Bowl 26

Tasty Dragon Fruit & Banana Smoothie Bowl 27

Fresh Avocado & Spinach Smoothie Bowl 27

Creamy Banana Rum Smoothie Bowl

⏰ **Prep: 10 minutes**   📚 **Serves: 2**

Ingredients:

½ of ripe banana, peeled and cut in ½-inch pieces
¼ cup rum
¼ cup heavy cream
½ cup whole milk
¾ cup apple juice
2 tablespoons fresh orange juice

Preparation:

1. In a large-sized bowl, put banana and remaining ingredients and whisk to incorporate thoroughly. 2. Transfer the blended mixture into an empty Ninja CREAMi pint container. 3. Cover the container with storage lid and freeze for 24 hours. 4. After 24 hours, take off the lid from container and arrange into the outer bowl of Ninja CREAMi. 5. Install the "Creamerizer Paddle" onto the lid of outer bowl. 6. Then rotate the lid clockwise to lock. 7. Press "Power" button to turn on the unit. 8. Then press "SMOOTHIE BOWL" button. 9. When the program is completed, turn the outer bowl and release it from the machine. 10. Transfer the smoothie into serving bowls and enjoy immediately.

Serving Suggestions: Serve with a topping of granola
Variation Tip: Make sure to use ripened banana.
Nutritional Information per Serving: Calories: 228|Fat: 7.8g|Sat Fat: 4.7g|Carbohydrates: 322g|Fiber: 1g|Sugar: 17.1g|Protein: 2.8g

Papaya and Banana Smoothie Bowl

⏰ **Prep: 10 minutes**   📚 **Serves: 2**

Ingredients:

4 ounces fresh papaya, peeled, pitted and cut up
2¾ ounces bananas, peeled and thinly sliced
5¼ ounces vanilla yogurt
3½ ounces coconut milk

Preparation:

1. In an empty Ninja CREAMi pint container, put the fruit slices. 2. Top with yogurt and milk. 3. Cover the container with storage lid and freeze for 24 hours. 4. After 24 hours, take off the lid from container and arrange into the outer bowl of Ninja CREAMi. 5. Install the "Creamerizer Paddle" onto the lid of outer bowl. 6. Then rotate the lid clockwise to lock. 7. Press "Power" button to turn on the unit. 8. Then press "SMOOTHIE BOWL" button. 9. When the program is completed, turn the outer bowl and release it from the machine. 10. Transfer the smoothie into serving bowls and enjoy immediately.

Serving Suggestions: Top with berries before serving.
Variation Tip: You can use non-dairy yogurt instead of regular yogurt.
Nutritional Information per Serving: Calories: 140 |Fat: 3g|Sat Fat: 1.9g|Carbohydrates: 22.9g|Fiber: 2.8g|Sugar: 15.4g|Protein: 6.7g

Honey Oats Tofu Smoothie Bowl

⏰ Prep: 10 minutes 🍳 Cook: 1 minute 🍽 Serves: 2

Ingredients:

½ cup unsweetened almond milk
¼ cup quick oats
1 cup Greek yogurt
½ cup tofu, pressed, drained and cut up
3 tablespoons honey

Preparation:

1. In a small microwave-safe bowl, put almond milk and oats and microwave on High or about 1 minute. 2. Take off from the microwave and blend in the yogurt, tofu and honey to incorporate thoroughly. 3. Transfer the mixture into an empty Ninja CREAMi pint container. 4. Cover the container with storage lid and freeze for 24 hours. 5. After 24 hours, take off the lid from container and arrange into the outer bowl of Ninja CREAMi. 6. Install the "Creamerizer Paddle" onto the lid of outer bowl. 7. Then rotate the lid clockwise to lock. 8. Press "Power" button to turn on the unit. 9. Then press "SMOOTHIE BOWL" button. 10. When the program is completed, turn the outer bowl and release it from the machine. 11. Transfer the smoothie into serving bowls and serve with your favorite topping.

Serving Suggestions: Serve with a topping of fresh fruit slices
Variation Tip: Make sure to drain tofu thoroughly.
Nutritional Information per Serving: Calories: 276 |Fat: 5.7g|Sat Fat: 2g|Carbohydrates: 43.1g|Fiber: 1.9g|Sugar: 35g|Protein: 13.8g

Nutritious Avocado Banana Smoothie Bowl

⏰ Prep: 10 minutes 🍽 Serves: 4

Ingredients:

2 tablespoons whey protein powder
¼ cup honey
¼ cup apple juice
½ cup whole milk
1 cup ripe banana, peeled and cut in ½-inch pieces
1 cup avocado, peeled, pitted and cut up

Preparation:

1. In a large bowl, put protein powder, honey, apple juice and milk and beat to incorporate thoroughly. 2. Place the banana and avocado into an empty Ninja CREAMi pint container and with the back of a spoon, firmly press the fruit below the MAX FILL line. 3. Top with milk mixture and blend to incorporate thoroughly. 4. Cover the container with storage lid and freeze for 24 hours. 5. After 24 hours, take off the lid from container and arrange into the outer bowl of Ninja CREAMi. 6. Install the "Creamerizer Paddle" onto the lid of outer bowl. 7. Then rotate the lid clockwise to lock. 8. Press "Power" button to turn on the unit. 9. Then press "SMOOTHIE BOWL" button. 10. When the program is completed, turn the outer bowl and release it from the machine. 11. Transfer the smoothie into serving bowls and serve immediately.

Serving Suggestions: Serve with a topping of coconut flakes.
Variation Tip: Make sure to use ripened avocado
Nutritional Information per Serving: Calories: 298 |Fat: 18.2g|Sat Fat: 14.8g|Carbohydrates: 35g|Fiber: 7.9g|Sugar: 16.2g|Protein: 9.9g

Tropical Mango Pineapple Smoothie Bowl

⏰ **Prep: 10 minutes** 📚 **Serves: 2**

▶ **Ingredients:**

2 cups frozen mango chunks
½ cup pineapple juice
1 tablespoon maple syrup

▶ **Preparation:**

1. In a high-powered blender, put in mango chunks and remaining ingredients and process to form a smooth mixture. 2. Transfer the blended mixture into an empty Ninja CREAMi pint container. 3. Cover the container with storage lid and freeze for 24 hours. 4. After 24 hours, take off the lid from container and arrange into the outer bowl of Ninja CREAMi. 5. Install the "Creamerizer Paddle" onto the lid of outer bowl. 6. Then rotate the lid clockwise to lock. 7. Press "Power" button to turn on the unit. 8. Then press "SMOOTHIE BOWL" button. 9. When the program is completed, turn the outer bowl and release it from the machine. 10. Transfer the smoothie into serving bowls and enjoy immediately.

Serving Suggestions: Serve with a topping of berries.
Variation Tip: you can adjust the ratio of sweetener according to your taste.
Nutritional Information per Serving: Calories: 125 |Fat: 0.7g|Sat Fat: 0g|Carbohydrates: 32.3g|Fiber: 6.9g|Sugar: 22.9g|Protein: 0.7g

Banana Berry Smoothie Bowl

⏰ **Prep: 10 minutes** 📚 **Serves: 4**

▶ **Ingredients:**

1 frozen banana, cut up
3 cups frozen berries
¼ cup full-fat coconut milk

▶ **Preparation:**

1. In a high-powered blender, put in banana and remaining ingredients and process to form a smooth mixture. 2. Transfer the blended mixture into an empty Ninja CREAMi pint container. 3. Cover the container with storage lid and freeze for 24 hours. 4. After 24 hours, take off the lid from container and arrange into the outer bowl of Ninja CREAMi. 5. Install the "Creamerizer Paddle" onto the lid of outer bowl. 6. Then rotate the lid clockwise to lock. 7. Press "Power" button to turn on the unit. 8. Then press "SMOOTHIE BOWL" button. 9. When the program is completed, turn the outer bowl and release it from the machine. 10. Transfer the smoothie into serving bowls and enjoy immediately.

Serving Suggestions: Serve with a topping shredded coconut.
Variation Tip: Use best quality berries.
Nutritional Information per Serving: Calories: 116 |Fat: 3.5g|Sat Fat: 2.8g|Carbohydrates: 20g|Fiber: 4.5g|Sugar: 11.4g|Protein: 1.3g

Citrus Blueberry Smoothie Bowl

⏰ **Prep: 10 minutes**   🍽 **Serves: 2**

Ingredients:

2 cups frozen blueberries
1 cup orange juice
⅓ cup honey
½ teaspoon ground cinnamon

Preparation:

1. In an empty Ninja CREAMi pint container, put in blueberries. 2. In a large-sized bowl, put in the orange juice, honey and cinnamon and whisk to incorporate thoroughly. 3. Place the blended mixture over the cherries and lightly blend to incorporate. 4. Cover the container with storage lid and freeze for 24 hours. 5. After 24 hours, take off the lid from container and arrange into the outer bowl of Ninja CREAMi. 6. Install the "Creamerizer Paddle" onto the lid of outer bowl. 7. Then rotate the lid clockwise to lock. 8. Press "Power" button to turn on the unit. 9. Then press "SMOOTHIE BOWL" button. 10. When the program is completed, turn the outer bowl and release it from the machine. 11. Transfer the smoothie into serving bowls and enjoy immediately.

Serving Suggestions: Serve with a topping of peanut butter.
Variation Tip: Use freshly squeezed orange juice.
Nutritional Information per Serving: Calories: 282 |Fat: 0.4g|Sat Fat: 0.1g|Carbohydrates: 66.9g|Fiber: 6.1g|Sugar: 57.5g|Protein: 0.6g

Easy Peach Smoothie Bowl

⏰ **Prep: 10 minutes**   🍽 **Serves: 4**

Ingredients:

2 cups peaches, pitted and cut into 1-inch pieces
14 ounces full-fat milk
2-3 drops liquid stevia

Preparation:

1. Place the peach pieces into an empty Ninja CREAMi pint container. 2. Top with milk and stevia and blend to incorporate. 3. Cover the container with storage lid and freeze for 24 hours. 4. After 24 hours, take off the lid from container and arrange into the outer bowl of Ninja CREAMi. 5. Install the "Creamerizer Paddle" onto the lid of outer bowl. 6. Then rotate the lid clockwise to lock. 7. Press "Power" button to turn on the unit. 8. Then press "SMOOTHIE BOWL" button. 9. When the program is completed, turn the outer bowl and release it from the machine. 10. Transfer the smoothie into serving bowls and enjoy immediately.

Serving Suggestions: Serve with a topping of walnuts.
Variation Tip: Make sure to use full-fat milk.
Nutritional Information per Serving: Calories: 92 |Fat: 3.5g|Sat Fat: 2.1g|Carbohydrates: 12g|Fiber: 1.2g|Sugar: 12g|Protein: 4g

Mango Banana Smoothie Bowl

⏱ **Prep: 10 minutes**   🍽 **Serves: 2**

Ingredients:

1 cup frozen mango chunks
1 fresh banana, peel removed and halved
½ teaspoon almond extract
⅛ teaspoon ground cinnamon
2 tablespoons coconut milk

Preparation:

1. In a high-powered blender, put in mango chunks and remaining ingredients and process to form a smooth mixture. 2. Transfer the blended mixture into an empty Ninja CREAMi pint container. 3. Cover the container with storage lid and freeze for 24 hours. 4. After 24 hours, take off the lid from container and arrange into the outer bowl of Ninja CREAMi. 5. Install the "Creamerizer Paddle" onto the lid of outer bowl. 6. Then rotate the lid clockwise to lock. 7. Press "Power" button to turn on the unit. 8. Then press "SMOOTHIE BOWL" button. 9. When the program is completed, turn the outer bowl and release it from the machine. 10. Transfer the smoothie into serving bowls and enjoy immediately.

Serving Suggestions: Serve with a topping of chopped nuts.
Variation Tip: You can adjust the ratio of cinnamon according to you taste.
Nutritional Information per Serving: Calories: 140 |Fat: 4.1g|Sat Fat: 3.3g|Carbohydrates: 26.9g|Fiber: 3.3g|Sugar: 19.1g|Protein: 1.7g

Sweet Potato and Banana Smoothie Bowl

⏱ **Prep: 10 minutes**   🍽 **Serves: 2**

Ingredients:

1 cup canned sweet potato puree
⅓ cup plain yogurt
1½ tablespoons honey
1 teaspoon vanilla extract
½ teaspoon ground cinnamon
¼ teaspoon ground nutmeg
¼ teaspoon ground ginger
1 frozen banana, peeled and cut in ½-inch pieces

Preparation:

1. In an empty Ninja CREAMi pint container, put sweet potato puree, yogurt, honey, vanilla extract, and spices and blend to incorporate thoroughly. 2. Add the banana pieces and blend to incorporate. 3. Transfer the mixture into an empty Ninja CREAMi pint container. 4. Arrange the container into the outer bowl of Ninja CREAMi. 5. Install the "Creamerizer Paddle" onto the lid of outer bowl. 6. Then rotate the lid clockwise to lock. 7. Press "Power" button to turn on the unit. 8. Then press "SMOOTHIE BOWL" button. 9. When the program is completed, turn the outer bowl and release it from the machine. 10. Transfer the smoothie into serving bowls and serve immediately.

Serving Suggestions: Serve with a sprinkling of cinnamon.
Variation Tip: You can use warm spices of your choice.
Nutritional Information per Serving: Calories: 170 | Fat: 0.7g|Sat Fat: 0.3g|Carbohydrates: 35.8g|Fiber: 5.2g|Sugar: 22g|Protein: 7.5g

Delicious Chocolate Banana Smoothie Bowl

⏰ **Prep: 10 minutes**   ◆ **Serves: 4**

> Ingredients:

½ cup chocolate almond milk
¼ cup fresh orange juice
2 tablespoons chocolate protein powder
3-4 tablespoons agave nectar
¼ teaspoon vanilla extract
2 cups bananas, peeled and cut in ½-inch pieces

> Preparation:

1. In a large-sized bowl, put in the almond milk, orange juice, protein powder, agave nectar and vanilla extract and whisk to incorporate thoroughly. 2. Place the banana pieces into an empty Ninja CREAMi pint container and with the back of a spoon, firmly press the fruit below the MAX FILL line. 3. Top with coconut milk mixture and blend to incorporate thoroughly. 4. Cover the container with storage lid and freeze for 24 hours. 5. After 24 hours, take off the lid from container and arrange into the outer bowl of Ninja CREAMi. 6. Install the "Creamerizer Paddle" onto the lid of outer bowl. 7. Then rotate the lid clockwise to lock. 8. Press "Power" button to turn on the unit. 9. Then press "SMOOTHIE BOWL" button. 10. When the program is completed, turn the outer bowl and release it from the machine. 11. Transfer the smoothie into serving bowls and enjoy immediately.

Serving Suggestions: Serve with a topping of chocolate chunks.
Variation Tip: Feel free to use sweetener of your choice.
Nutritional Information per Serving: Calories: 324 |Fat: 7.9g|Sat Fat: 2.5g|Carbohydrates: 52.2g|Fiber: 2.8g|Sugar: 49g|Protein: 19.1g

Honeyed Strawberry-Banana Smoothie Bowl

⏰ **Prep: 10 minutes**   ◆ **Serves: 2**

> Ingredients:

1 cup fresh strawberries, hulled and sliced
1 cup ripe banana, peel removed and sliced
14 ounces unsweetened almond milk
2-3 tablespoons honey
¼ teaspoon vanilla extract

> Preparation:

1. Place the strawberry and banana slices into an empty Ninja CREAMi pint container. 2. Top with coconut milk, honey and vanilla extract and blend to incorporate. 3. Cover the container with the storage lid and freeze for 24 hours. 4. After 24 hours, take off the lid from container and arrange into the outer bowl of Ninja CREAMi. 5. Install the "Creamerizer Paddle" onto the lid of outer bowl. 6. Then rotate the lid clockwise to lock. 7. Press "Power" button to turn on the unit. 8. Then press "SMOOTHIE BOWL" button. 9. When the program is completed, turn the outer bowl and release it from the machine. 10. Transfer the smoothie into serving bowls and enjoy immediately.

Serving Suggestions: Serve with a topping of chia seeds.
Variation Tip: Use fresh and ripe strawberries.
Nutritional Information per Serving: Calories: 187 |Fat: 3.3g|Sat Fat: 0.3g|Carbohydrates: 41.6g|Fiber: 4.2g|Sugar: 30g|Protein: 2.2g

Chia Banana Smoothie Bowl

⏰ **Prep: 10 minutes** 📚 **Serves: 2**

Ingredients:

2 frozen bananas, peel removed
2 tablespoons almond butter
2 tablespoons chia seeds
½ teaspoon vanilla extract
¼ cup whole milk

Preparation:

1. In a high-powered blender, put in bananas and remaining ingredients and process to form a smooth mixture. 2. Transfer the blended mixture into an empty Ninja CREAMi pint container. 3. Cover the container with storage lid and freeze for 24 hours. 4. After 24 hours, take off the lid from container and arrange into the outer bowl of Ninja CREAMi. 5. Install the "Creamerizer Paddle" onto the lid of outer bowl. 6. Then rotate the lid clockwise to lock. 7. Press "Power" button to turn on the unit. 8. Then press "SMOOTHIE BOWL" button. 9. When the program is completed, turn the outer bowl and release it from the machine. 10. Transfer the smoothie into serving bowls and enjoy immediately.

Serving Suggestions: Serve with a topping of fresh fruit.
Variation Tip: Make sure to use ripened banana.
Nutritional Information per Serving: Calories: 253 |Fat: 12.9g|Sat Fat: 1.6g|Carbohydrates: 34.5g|Fiber: 7.2g|Sugar: 16.9g|Protein: 7.2g

Orange Peach Smoothie Bowl

⏰ **Prep: 10 minutes** 📚 **Serves: 4**

Ingredients:

1 cup frozen peach chunks
1 cup plain yogurt
¼ cup fresh orange juice
2 tablespoons honey
⅓ teaspoon vanilla extract

Preparation:

1. In a high-powered blender, put in peach chunks and remaining ingredients and process to form a smooth mixture. 2. Transfer the blended mixture into an empty Ninja CREAMi pint container. 3. Cover the container with storage lid and freeze for 24 hours. 4. After 24 hours, take off the lid from container and arrange into the outer bowl of Ninja CREAMi. 5. Install the "Creamerizer Paddle" onto the lid of outer bowl. 6. Then rotate the lid clockwise to lock. 7. Press "Power" button to turn on the unit. 8. Then press "SMOOTHIE BOWL" button. 9. When the program is completed, turn the outer bowl and release it from the machine. 10. Transfer the smoothie into serving bowls and enjoy immediately.

Serving Suggestions: Serve with a garnishing of fresh peach slices.
Variation Tip: Feel free to use non-dairy yogurt.
Nutritional Information per Serving: Calories: 197 |Fat: 1.8g|Sat Fat: 1.2g|Carbohydrates: 36.2g|Fiber: 1.3g|Sugar: 35.6g|Protein: 8g

Tropical Yogurt Smoothie Bowl

⏰ **Prep: 10 minutes**   📚 **Serves: 2**

Ingredients:

¾ cup fresh mango, peel removed, pitted and cut up
¾ cup fresh pineapple, peel removed and cut up
½ cup fresh papaya, peel removed and cut up
½ cup coconut yogurt
¼ cup fresh orange juice
1 tablespoon agave nectar
½ teaspoon vanilla extract

Preparation:

1. In an empty Ninja CREAMi pint container, put in fruit pieces and with the back of a spoon, firmly press below the MAX FILL line. 2. Put in yogurt, orange juice, agave nectar and vanilla extract and blend to incorporate. 3. Cover the container with storage lid and freeze for 24 hours. 4. After 24 hours, take off the lid from container and arrange into the outer bowl of Ninja CREAMi. 5. Install the "Creamerizer Paddle" onto the lid of outer bowl. 6. Then rotate the lid clockwise to lock. 7. Press "Power" button to turn on the unit. 8. Then press "SMOOTHIE BOWL" button. 9. When the program is completed, turn the outer bowl and release it from the machine. 10. Transfer the smoothie into serving bowls and enjoy immediately.
Serving Suggestions: Serve with a topping of fresh berries.
Variation Tip: Coconut yogurt can be replaced with Greek yogurt.
Nutritional Information per Serving: Calories: 176 |Fat: 1.2g|Sat Fat: 0.7g|Carbohydrates: 37.6g|Fiber: 2.6g|Sugar: 33g|Protein: 4.8g

Quick Raspberry Yogurt Smoothie Bowl

⏰ **Prep: 10 minutes**   📚 **Serves: 2**

Ingredients:

1 cup frozen raspberries
1 cup plain yogurt
¼ cup fresh orange juice
2 tablespoons agave nectar
¼ teaspoon vanilla extract

Preparation:

1. In a high-powered blender, put in raspberries and remaining ingredients and process to form a smooth mixture. 2. Transfer the blended mixture into an empty Ninja CREAMi pint container. 3. Cover the container with storage lid and freeze for 24 hours. 4. After 24 hours, take off the lid from container and arrange into the outer bowl of Ninja CREAMi. 5. Install the "Creamerizer Paddle" onto the lid of outer bowl. 6. Then rotate the lid clockwise to lock. 7. Press "Power" button to turn on the unit. 8. Then press "SMOOTHIE BOWL" button. 9. When the program is completed, turn the outer bowl and release it from the machine. 10. Transfer the smoothie into serving bowls and enjoy immediately.
Serving Suggestions: Serve with a topping of pomegranate seeds.
Variation Tip: Orange juice can be replaced with apple juice.
Nutritional Information per Serving: Calories: 291 |Fat: 1.8g|Sat Fat: 1.3g|Carbohydrates: 60.6g|Fiber: 6.6g|Sugar:53.5g|Protein: 8.1g

Tasty Dragon Fruit & Banana Smoothie Bowl

Prep: 10 minutes   Serves: 4

Ingredients:
1 cup dragon fruit, peel removed and cut up
1 large banana, peel removed and sliced
1 cup brewed coffee
½ cup whole milk
2 tablespoons peanut butter

Preparation:
1. In a high-powered blender, put in dragon fruit and remaining ingredients and process to form a smooth mixture. 2. Transfer the blended mixture into an empty Ninja CREAMi pint container. 3. Cover the container with storage lid and freeze for 24 hours. 4. After 24 hours, take off the lid from container and arrange into the outer bowl of Ninja CREAMi. 5. Install the "Creamerizer Paddle" onto the lid of outer bowl. 6. Then rotate the lid clockwise to lock. 7. Press "Power" button to turn on the unit. 8. Then press "SMOOTHIE BOWL" button. 9. When the program is completed, turn the outer bowl and release it from the machine. 10. Transfer the smoothie into serving bowls and enjoy immediately.
Serving Suggestions: Serve with a garnishing of coconut flakes.
Variation Tip: Use cold brewed coffee.
Nutritional Information per Serving: Calories: 103 |Fat: 5.1g|Sat Fat: 1.5g|Carbohydrates: 12.7g|Fiber: 1.3g|Sugar: 9g|Protein: 3.4g

Fresh Avocado & Spinach Smoothie Bowl

Prep: 10 minutes   Serves: 4

Ingredients:
½ cup full-fat coconut milk
¼ cup fresh pineapple juice
2 tablespoons whey protein powder
4 tablespoons agave nectar
¼ teaspoon vanilla extract
1½ cups avocado, peel removed, pitted and cut in ½-inch pieces
½ cup fresh spinach, cut up

Preparation:
1. In a large-sized bowl, put in coconut milk, pineapple juice, whey protein powder, agave nectar and vanilla extract and whisk to incorporate thoroughly. 2. Place the avocado and spinach into an empty Ninja CREAMi pint container and with the back of a spoon, firmly press the fruit below the MAX FILL line. 3. Top with coconut milk mixture and mix until blended thoroughly. 4. Cover the container with storage lid and freeze for 24 hours. 5. After 24 hours, take off the lid from container and arrange into the outer bowl of Ninja CREAMi. 6. Install the "Creamerizer Paddle" onto the lid of outer bowl. 7. Then rotate the lid clockwise to lock. 8. Press "Power" button to turn on the unit. 9. Then press "SMOOTHIE BOWL" button. 10. When the program is completed, turn the outer bowl and release it from the machine. 11. Transfer the smoothie into serving bowls and enjoy immediately.
Serving Suggestions: Serve with a topping of fresh raspberries.
Variation Tip: Avocado can be replaced with banana.
Nutritional Information per Serving: Calories: 265 |Fat: 18.1g|Sat Fat: 8.7g|Carbohydrates: 25g|Fiber: 5.5g|Sugar: 18g|Protein: 4.6g

Chapter 3 Ice Creams

Creamy Banana Ice Cream 29
Sweet Blackberry Ice Cream 29
Cheesy Strawberry Pudding Ice Cream 30
Mouthwatering Coconut Pineapple Ice Cream 30
Homemade Chocolate Ice Cream 31
Perfect Matcha Pudding Ice Cream 31
Vanilla Mango Ice Cream 32
Citrus Peach Ice Cream 32
Creamy Coffee Ice Cream 33
Boozy Orange Ice Cream 33
Simple Banana & Strawberry Yogurt Ice Cream 34
Sweet Mango Ice Cream 34
Limey Honeydew Melon Ice Cream 35
Delicious Blue Spirulina Ice Cream 35
Creamy Rum Ice Cream 36
Lemony Apple Ice Cream 36
Easy Vanilla Cocoa Ice Cream 37
Best Lavender Tea Ice Cream 37

Creamy Banana Ice Cream

⏰ **Prep: 10 minutes** 📚 **Serves: 4**

Ingredients:

1 cup whole milk
¾ cup heavy cream
2 tablespoons tahini
½ banana, peeled
1 teaspoon vanilla extract
¼ cup honey

Preparation:

1. In a high-powered blender, put milk and remaining ingredients and process to form a smooth mixture. 2. Transfer the blended mixture into an empty Ninja CREAMi pint container. 3. Cover the container with storage lid and freeze for 24 hours. 4. After 24 hours, take off the lid from container and arrange into the outer bowl of Ninja CREAMi. 5. Install the "Creamerizer Paddle" onto the lid of outer bowl. 6. Then rotate the lid clockwise to lock. 7. Press "Power" button to turn on the unit. 8. Then press "ICE CREAM" button. 9. When the program is completed, turn the outer bowl and release it from the machine. 10. Transfer the ice cream into serving bowls and enjoy immediately.

Serving Suggestions: Serve with a topping of chopped peanuts.
Variation Tip: Swap the maple syrup with honey.
Nutritional Information per Serving: Calories: 229 |Fat: 14.4g|Sat Fat: 7.2g|Carbohydrates: 21.7g|Fiber: 0.9g|Sugar: 17.6g|Protein: 4.6g

Sweet Blackberry Ice Cream

⏰ **Prep: 10 minutes** 📚 **Serves: 4**

Ingredients:

1 cup heavy cream
1½ cups fresh blackberries, peeled and sliced
3 tablespoons white sugar
1 teaspoon vanilla extract

Preparation:

1. In a bowl, put heavy cream and whisk to form a smooth mixture. 2. Add the blackberries and with the back of a fork, lightly mash them. 3. Add in the sugar and vanilla extract and stir to incorporate thoroughly. 4. Transfer the blended mixture into an empty Ninja CREAMi pint container. 5. Cover the container with storage lid and freeze for 24 hours. 6. After 24 hours, take off the lid from container and arrange into the outer bowl of Ninja CREAMi. 7. Install the "Creamerizer Paddle" onto the lid of outer bowl. 8. Then rotate the lid clockwise to lock. 9. Press "Power" button to turn on the unit. 10. Then press "ICE CREAM" button. 11. When the program is completed, turn the outer bowl and release it from the machine. 12. Transfer the ice cream into serving bowls and enjoy immediately.

Serving Suggestions: Serve with a topping of caramel sauce.
Variation Tip: You can replace banana extract with vanilla extract.
Nutritional Information per Serving: Calories: 191 |Fat: 14.5g|Sat Fat: 12.7g|Carbohydrates: 16.3g|Fiber: 2.8g|Sugar: 9g|Protein: 2g

Cheesy Strawberry Pudding Ice Cream

⏱ Prep: 10 minutes   ≋ Serves: 4

Ingredients:

1 cup cottage cheese
½ cup milk
4 tablespoons instant strawberry pudding mix
2 tablespoons heavy cream
1 tablespoon honey
½ teaspoon vanilla extract

Preparation:

1. Place cottage cheese and remaining ingredients into a large-sized bowl and with an immersion blender, blend to incorporate. 2. Transfer the blended mixture into an empty Ninja CREAMi pint container. 3. Cover the container with storage lid and freeze for 24 hours. 4. After 24 hours, take off the lid from container and arrange into the outer bowl of Ninja CREAMi. 5. Install the "Creamerizer Paddle" onto the lid of outer bowl. 6. Then rotate the lid clockwise to lock. 7. Press "Power" button to turn on the unit. 8. Then press "ICE CREAM" button. 9. When the program is completed, turn the outer bowl and release it from the machine. 10. Transfer the ice cream into serving bowls and enjoy immediately.

Serving Suggestions: Serve with a topping of fresh strawberries.
Variation Tip: Vanilla extract can be replaced with almond extract too.
Nutritional Information per Serving: Calories: 215 |Fat: 6.4g|Sat Fat: 3.9g|Carbohydrates: 27.2g|Fiber: 0.6g|Sugar: 4.7g|Protein: 12.7g

Mouthwatering Coconut Pineapple Ice Cream

Prep: 10 minutes   Cook: 5 minutes   Serves: 4

Ingredients:

1 cup fresh pineapple, peel removed and roughly cut up
¼ cup granulated sugar
1 cup full-fat coconut milk
½ cup coconut cream

Preparation:

1. In a small-sized saucepan, put in pineapple and sugar and blend to incorporate. 2. Place the pan of pineapple on burner at around medium heat. 3. Cook for around 3-5 minutes, stirring occasionally. 4. Take off the pan of pineapple from burner and transfer in to a small-sized bowl. 5. Put it aside to cool for a few minutes. 6. In the bowl of pineapple, put in coconut milk and coconut cream and with an immersion blender, blend to form a smooth mixture. 7. Transfer the blended mixture into an empty Ninja CREAMi pint container. 8. Cover the container with storage lid and freeze for 24 hours. 9. After 24 hours, take off the lid from container and arrange into the outer bowl of Ninja CREAMi. 10. Install the "Creamerizer Paddle" onto the lid of outer bowl. 11. Then rotate the lid clockwise to lock. 12. Press "Power" button to turn on the unit. 13. Then press "ICE CREAM" button. 14. When the program is completed, turn the outer bowl and release it from the machine. 15. Transfer the ice cream into serving bowls and enjoy immediately.

Serving Suggestions: Serve with a topping of coconut cream.
Variation Tip: You can use dairy cream in this recipe
Nutritional Information per Serving: Calories: 161 |Fat: 7.5g|Sat Fat: 4.7g|Carbohydrates: 20.9g|Fiber: 0.6g|Sugar: 21.5g|Protein: 2.3g

Homemade Chocolate Ice Cream

⏰ **Prep: 15 minutes**   🍲 **Cook: 10 seconds**   ❖ **Serves: 4**

🟢 Ingredients:

1 tablespoon cream cheese, softened
⅓ cup granulated sugar
2 tablespoons cocoa powder
1 teaspoon vanilla extract
1 cup whole milk
¾ cup heavy cream

🟢 Preparation:

1. In a large microwave-safe bowl, put cream cheese and microwave for on High for around 10 seconds. 2. Take off from the microwave and stir to form a smooth mixture. 3. Add the sugar, cocoa powder and vanilla extract and with a wire whisk, beat until the mixture looks like frosting. 4. Slowly add the milk and heavy cream and beat to incorporate thoroughly. 5. Transfer the mixture into an empty Ninja CREAMi pint container. 6. Cover the container with storage lid and freeze for 24 hours. 7. After 24 hours, take off the lid from container and arrange into the outer bowl of Ninja CREAMi. 8. Install the "Creamerizer Paddle" onto the lid of outer bowl. 9. Then rotate the lid clockwise to lock. 10. Press "Power" button to turn on the unit. 11. Then press "ICE CREAM" button. 12. When the program is completed, turn the outer bowl and release it from the machine. 13. Transfer the ice cream into serving bowls and serve immediately.

Serving Suggestions: Serve with the topping of chopped nuts.
Variation Tip: Use high quality cocoa powder.
Nutritional Information per Serving: Calories: 188 | Fat: 11.2g|Sat Fat: 6.9g|Carbohydrates: 20.3g|Fiber: 0g|Sugar: 20g|Protein: 2.6g

Perfect Matcha Pudding Ice Cream

⏰ **Prep: 10 minutes**   ❖ **Serves: 4**

🟢 Ingredients:

1 (11.5 ounce) bottle vanilla protein shake
¼ cup whole milk
2 tablespoons instant vanilla pudding mix
1¼ tablespoons matcha powder

🟢 Preparation:

1. In a large-sized bowl, put in protein shake and remaining ingredients and blend to incorporate. 2. Transfer the blended mixture into an empty Ninja CREAMi pint container. 3. Cover the container with storage lid and freeze for 24 hours. 4. After 24 hours, take off the lid from container and arrange into the outer bowl of Ninja CREAMi. 5. Install the "Creamerizer Paddle" onto the lid of outer bowl. 6. Then rotate the lid clockwise to lock. 7. Press "Power" button to turn on the unit. 8. Then press "LITE ICE CREAM" button. 9. When the program is completed, turn the outer bowl and release it from the machine. 10. Transfer the ice cream into serving bowls and enjoy immediately.

Serving Suggestions: Serve with a topping of chocolate sprinkles.
Variation Tip: you can use shake of your choice.
Nutritional Information per Serving: Calories: 393 |Fat: 7.1g|Sat Fat: 3.8g|Carbohydrates: 50.6g|Fiber: 0.9g|Sugar: 36.4g|Protein: 34.8g

Vanilla Mango Ice Cream

⏲ **Prep:** 10 minutes 📚 **Serves:** 4

Ingredients:

1 cup whole milk
1¼ cups frozen mango chunks
1 teaspoon vanilla extract

Preparation:

1. In a high-powered blender, put milk and remaining ingredients and process to form a smooth mixture. 2. Transfer the blended mixture into an empty Ninja CREAMi pint container. 3. Cover the container with storage lid and freeze for 24 hours. 4. After 24 hours, take off the lid from container and arrange into the outer bowl of Ninja CREAMi. 5. Install the "Creamerizer Paddle" onto the lid of outer bowl. 6. Then rotate the lid clockwise to lock. 7. Press "Power" button to turn on the unit. 8. Then press "ICE CREAM" button. 9. When the program is completed, turn the outer bowl and release it from the machine. 10. Transfer the ice cream into serving bowls and enjoy immediately.

Serving Suggestions: Serve with a topping of chocolate chips.
Variation Tip: You can use almond extract instead of vanilla extract.
Nutritional Information per Serving: Calories: 155 |Fat: 12.3g|Sat Fat: 11.1g|Carbohydrates: 10.5g|Fiber: 2.8g|Sugar: 5.9g|Protein: 1.6g

Citrus Peach Ice Cream

⏲ **Prep:** 15 minutes 📚 **Serves:** 4

Ingredients:

¾ cup heavy cream
½ cup milk
⅓ cup orange juice
¾ cup sugar
½ cup frozen peach chunks

Preparation:

1. In a bowl, put heavy cream, milk, orange juice and sugar and beat until sugar is dissolved. 2. In an empty Ninja CREAMi pint container, put the peach chunks and top with milk mixture. 3. Cover the container with storage lid and freeze for 24 hours. 4. After 24 hours, take off the lid from container and arrange into the outer bowl of Ninja CREAMi. 5. Install the "Creamerizer Paddle" onto the lid of outer bowl. 6. Then rotate the lid clockwise to lock. 7. Press "Power" button to turn on the unit. 8. Then press "ICE CREAM" button. 9. When the program is completed, turn the outer bowl and release it from the machine. 10. Transfer the ice cream into serving bowls and serve immediately.

Serving Suggestions: Serve with the garnishing of orange zest.
Variation Tip: For best result, use ripe peaches.
Nutritional Information per Serving: Calories: 250 | Fat: 9g|Sat Fat: 5.6g|Carbohydrates: 43.5g|Fiber: 0.3g|Sugar: 41.8g|Protein: 1.7g

Creamy Coffee Ice Cream

⏰ **Prep: 10 minutes** 🍳 **Cook: 10 seconds** 🍽 **Serves: 4**

▸ **Ingredients:**

1 tablespoon cream cheese, softened
⅓ cup granulated sugar
1 teaspoon vanilla extract
2 tablespoons instant coffee powder
1 cup whole milk
¾ cup heavy cream

▸ **Preparation:**

1. In a large-sized microwave-safe bowl, put cream cheese and microwave on High for around 10 seconds. 2. Take off from the microwave and stir to form a smooth mixture. 3. Add the sugar and vanilla extract and with a wire whisk, whisk until the mixture looks like frosting. 4. Slowly add the coffee powder, milk and heavy cream and whisk to incorporate thoroughly. 5. Transfer the blended mixture into an empty Ninja CREAMi pint container. 6. Cover the container with storage lid and freeze for 24 hours. 7. After 24 hours, take off the lid from container and arrange into the outer bowl of Ninja CREAMi. 8. Install the "Creamerizer Paddle" onto the lid of outer bowl. 9. Then rotate the lid clockwise to lock. 10. Press "Power" button to turn on the unit. 11. Then press "ICE CREAM" button. 12. When the program is completed, turn the outer bowl and release it from the machine. 13. Transfer the ice cream into serving bowls and enjoy immediately.

Serving Suggestions: Serve with a topping of chocolate shavings.
Variation Tip: You can also use espresso powder.
Nutritional Information per Serving: Calories: 319 |Fat: 26.3g|Sat Fat: 23g|Carbohydrates: 23.5g|Fiber: 3.1g|Sugar: 19.7g|Protein: 3.1g

Boozy Orange Ice Cream

⏰ **Prep: 10 minutes** 🍽 **Serves: 4**

▸ **Ingredients:**

¼ cup orange marmalade
2 tablespoons granulated sugar
2 tablespoons cirrus vodka
1 cup heavy cream
¼ cup whole milk
1 teaspoon orange zest, grated

▸ **Preparation:**

1. In a large-sized bowl, put in orange marmalade, sugar and vodka and whisk to incorporate thoroughly. 2. Put in heavy cream, milk, and orange zest and whisk to incorporate thoroughly. 3. Transfer the blended mixture into an empty Ninja CREAMi pint container. 4. Cover the container with storage lid and freeze for 24 hours. 5. After 24 hours, take off the lid from container and arrange into the outer bowl of Ninja CREAMi. 6. Install the "Creamerizer Paddle" onto the lid of outer bowl. 7. Then rotate the lid clockwise to lock. 8. Press "Power" button to turn on the unit. 9. Then press "ICE CREAM" button. 10. When the program is completed, turn the outer bowl and release it from the machine. 11. Transfer the ice cream into serving bowls and enjoy immediately.

Serving Suggestions: Serve with a topping of orange zest.
Variation Tip: Use high-quality orange marmalade.
Nutritional Information per Serving: Calories: 354 |Fat: 18.9g|Sat Fat: 11.1g|Carbohydrates: 15g|Fiber: 1.2g|Sugar: 12.9g|Protein: 4.1g

Simple Banana & Strawberry Yogurt Ice Cream

⏱ **Prep: 10 minutes**   📚 **Serves: 4**

Ingredients:

1 cup strawberry yogurt
¼ cup honey
1 tablespoon cream cheese, softened
1 teaspoon vanilla extract
2 bananas, peel removed and sliced

Preparation:

1. In a large-sized bowl, put in strawberry yogurt, honey, cream cheese and vanilla extract and whisk to incorporate thoroughly. 2. Add the banana slices and blend to incorporate. 3. Transfer the blended mixture into an empty Ninja CREAMi pint container. 4. Cover the container with storage lid and freeze for 24 hours. 5. After 24 hours, take off the lid from container and arrange into the outer bowl of Ninja CREAMi. 6. Install the "Creamerizer Paddle" onto the lid of outer bowl. 7. Then rotate the lid clockwise to lock. 8. Press "Power" button to turn on the unit. 9. Then press "ICE CREAM" button. 10. When the program is completed, turn the outer bowl and release it from the machine. 11. Transfer the ice cream into serving bowls and enjoy immediately.

Serving Suggestions: Serve with a garnishing of fresh strawberry slices.
Variation Tip: Use the best quality strawberry yogurt.
Nutritional Information per Serving: Calories: 189 |Fat: 1.8g|Sat Fat: 1.1g|Carbohydrates: 42.6g|Fiber: 1.6g|Sugar:36.2g|Protein: 3.3g

Sweet Mango Ice Cream

⏱ **Prep: 10 minutes**   📚 **Serves: 4**

Ingredients:

1 cup fresh mango, peel removed, pitted and roughly cut up
¼ cup granulated sugar
1 cup whole milk
½ cup heavy whipping cream

Preparation:

1. In a small-sized saucepan, put in mango and sugar and blend to incorporate. 2. Place the pan of mango on burner at around medium heat. 3. Cook for around 3-5 minutes, stirring occasionally. 4. Take off the pan of mango from burner and transfer in to a small-sized bowl. 5. Put it aside to cool for a few minutes. 6. In the bowl of mango, put in milk and heavy whipping cream and with an immersion blender, blend to form a smooth mixture. 7. Transfer the blended mixture into an empty Ninja CREAMi pint container. 8. Cover the container with storage lid and freeze for 24 hours. 9. After 24 hours, take off the lid from container and arrange into the outer bowl of Ninja CREAMi. 10. Install the "Creamerizer Paddle" onto the lid of outer bowl. 11. Then rotate the lid clockwise to lock. 12. Press "Power" button to turn on the unit. 13. Then press "ICE CREAM" button. 14. When the program is completed, turn the outer bowl and release it from the machine. 15. Transfer the ice cream into serving bowls and enjoy immediately.

Serving Suggestions: Serve with a topping of coconut cream.
Variation Tip: Use ripened mango.
Nutritional Information per Serving: Calories: 160 |Fat: 7.7g|Sat Fat: 4.6g|Carbohydrates: 21.9g|Fiber: 0.7g|Sugar:21.4g|Protein: 2.6g

Limey Honeydew Melon Ice Cream

⏱ **Prep: 10 minutes**   📚 **Serves: 4**

Ingredients:

2 cups honeydew melon, peel removed, seeded and cubed
2 tablespoons fresh lime juice
3 tablespoons honey

Preparation:

1. In an empty Ninja CREAMi pint container, put in honeydew melon cubes. 2. Top with the lime juice and honey and lightly blend to incorporate. 3. Arrange the container into the outer bowl of Ninja CREAMi. 4. Cover the container with storage lid and freeze for 24 hours. 5. After 24 hours, take off the lid from container and arrange into the outer bowl of Ninja CREAMi. 6. Install the "Creamerizer Paddle" onto the lid of outer bowl. 7. Then rotate the lid clockwise to lock. 8. Press "Power" button to turn on the unit. 9. Then press "ICE CREAM" button. 10. When the program is completed, turn the outer bowl and release it from the machine. 11. Transfer the ice cream into serving bowls and enjoy immediately.

Serving Suggestions: Serve with a garnishing of fresh mint leaves.
Variation Tip: For bright green color, you can use 2-3 drops of green food coloring.
Nutritional Information per Serving: Calories: 63 |Fat: 0g|Sat Fat: 0g|Carbohydrates: 16.6g|Fiber: 0g|Sugar: 12.9g|Protein: 0.1g

Delicious Blue Spirulina Ice Cream

⏱ **Prep: 15 minutes**   🍳 **Cook: 10 seconds**   📚 **Serves: 4**

Ingredients:

1 tablespoon cream cheese, softened
⅓ cup granulated sugar
2 tablespoons blue spirulina powder
1 teaspoon vanilla extract
1 cup unsweetened almond milk
¾ cup heavy cream

Preparation:

1. In a large microwave-safe bowl, put in cream cheese and microwave for on High for around 10 seconds. 2. Remove from the microwave and stir until smooth. 3. Add the sugar, blue spirulina powder and vanilla extract and with a wire whisk, beat until the mixture looks like frosting. 4. Slowly add the almond milk and heavy cream and whisk to incorporate thoroughly. 5. Transfer the mixture into an empty Ninja CREAMi pint container. 6. Cover the container with storage lid and freeze for 24 hours. 7. After 24 hours, take off the lid from container and arrange into the outer bowl of Ninja CREAMi. 8. Install the "Creamerizer Paddle" onto the lid of outer bowl. 9. Then rotate the lid clockwise to lock. 10. Press "Power" button to turn on the unit. 11. Then press "ICE CREAM" button. 12. When the program is completed, turn the outer bowl and release it from the machine. 13. Transfer the ice cream into serving bowls and serve immediately.

Serving Suggestions: Serve with a garnishing o fresh fruit.
Variation Tip: You can use dairy milk in this recipe.
Nutritional Information per Serving: Calories: 172 |Fat: 10.4g|Sat Fat: 5.9g|Carbohydrates:18.8g|Fiber:0.4g|Sugar:16.9g|Protein: 2.9g

Creamy Rum Ice Cream

⏰ Prep: 10 minutes   ≋ Serves: 4

Ingredients:

1 (14-ounce) can sweetened condensed milk
1¼ cups heavy cream
½ teaspoons sea salt flakes
2 tablespoons rum

Preparation:

1. In a large-sized bowl, place the condensed milk, cream and sea salt flakes and with a hand mixer, whisk until mixture becomes thick. 2. Add in the rum and gently stir to blend. 3. Transfer the blended mixture into an empty Ninja CREAMi pint container. 4. Cover the container with storage lid and freeze for 24 hours. 5. After 24 hours, take off the lid from container and arrange into the outer bowl of Ninja CREAMi. 6. Install the "Creamerizer Paddle" onto the lid of outer bowl. 7. Then rotate the lid clockwise to lock. 8. Press "Power" button to turn on the unit. 9. Then press "ICE CREAM" button. 10. When the program is completed, turn the outer bowl and release it from the machine. 11. Transfer the ice cream into serving bowls and enjoy immediately.
Serving Suggestions: Serve this ice cream alongside warm brownies.
Variation Tip: Condensed milk can be replaced with dulce de leche.
Nutritional Information per Serving: Calories: 464 |Fat: 22.5g|Sat Fat: 14.1g|Carbohydrates: 55g|Fiber: 0g|Sugar: 54g|Protein: 8.6g

Lemony Apple Ice Cream

Prep: 10 minutes   ≋ Serves: 4

Ingredients:

1 cup heavy cream
½ cup whole milk
½ cup apple juice
1 teaspoon vanilla extract
⅓ cup granulated sugar
½ teaspoon ground cinnamon
¼ teaspoon ground allspice
⅛ teaspoon ground nutmeg
⅛ teaspoon ground cloves
2 teaspoons lemon zest, grated

Preparation:

1. In a large-sized bowl, put in heavy cream and remaining ingredients and whisk to incorporate thoroughly. 2. Transfer the blended mixture into an empty Ninja CREAMi pint container. 3. Cover the container with storage lid and freeze for 24 hours. 4. After 24 hours, take off the lid from container and arrange into the outer bowl of Ninja CREAMi. 5. Install the "Creamerizer Paddle" onto the lid of outer bowl. 6. Then rotate the lid clockwise to lock. 7. Press "Power" button to turn on the unit. 8. Then press "ICE CREAM" button. 9. When the program is completed, turn the outer bowl and release it from the machine. 10. Transfer the ice cream into serving bowls and enjoy immediately.
Serving Suggestions: Serve with a drizzling of chocolate sauce.
Variation Tip: Feel free to adjust the ratio of spices.
Nutritional Information per Serving: Calories: 204 |Fat: 12.2g|Sat Fat: 7.5g|Carbohydrates: 23.1g|Fiber: 0.3g|Sugar:21.5g|Protein: 1.7g

Easy Vanilla Cocoa Ice Cream

⏱ Prep: 10 minutes   🍱 Cook: 10 seconds   🍽 Serves: 4

Ingredients:

1 tablespoon cream cheese, softened
⅓ cup granulated sugar
1 teaspoon vanilla extract
2 tablespoons cocoa powder
1 cup whole milk
¾ cup heavy cream

Preparation:

1. In a large-sized microwave-safe bowl, put in cream cheese and microwave on High for around 10 seconds. 2. Remove from the microwave and stir until smooth. 3. Add the sugar, cocoa powder and vanilla extract and with a wire whisk, whisk until the mixture looks like frosting. 4. Slowly add the milk and heavy cream and whisk to incorporate thoroughly. 5. Transfer the blended mixture into an empty Ninja CREAMi pint container. 6. Cover the container with storage lid and freeze for 24 hours. 7. After 24 hours, take off the lid from container and arrange into the outer bowl of Ninja CREAMi. 8. Install the "Creamerizer Paddle" onto the lid of outer bowl. 9. Then rotate the lid clockwise to lock. 10. Press "Power" button to turn on the unit. 11. Then press "ICE CREAM" button. 12. When the program is completed, turn the outer bowl and release it from the machine. 13. Transfer the ice cream into serving bowls and enjoy immediately.

Serving Suggestions: Serve with a garnishing of fresh raspberries.
Variation Tip: Cocoa powder can be replaced with cacao powder.
Nutritional Information per Serving: Calories: 194 |Fat: 11.5g|Sat Fat: 7.1g|Carbohydrates: 21.7g|Fiber: 0.8g|Sugar: 20.1g|Protein: 3.1g

Best Lavender Tea Ice Cream

⏱ Prep: 15 minutes   🍱 Cook: 25 minutes   🍽 Serves: 4

Ingredients:

1 cup heavy cream
1 cup whole milk
5 tablespoons white sugar
3 lavender tea bags
2-3 drops purple food coloring

Preparation:

1. In a medium saucepan, put in cream and milk and blend to incorporate. 2. Place saucepan on burner at around medium heat. 3. Cook for around 2-3 minutes or until steam is rising. 4. Blend in the sugar and reduce the heat to very low. 5. Add tea bags and cover the saucepan for around 20 minutes. 6. Discard the tea bags and remove saucepan from burner. 7. Transfer the mixture into an empty Ninja CREAMi pint container and place into an ice bath to cool. 8. After cooling, lend in the food coloring. 9. Cover the container with storage lid and freeze for 24 hours. 10. After 24 hours, take off the lid from container and arrange into the outer bowl of Ninja CREAMi. 11. Install the "Creamerizer Paddle" onto the lid of outer bowl. 12. Then rotate the lid clockwise to lock. 13. Press "Power" button to turn on the unit. 14. Then press "ICE CREAM" button. 15. When the program is completed, turn the outer bowl and release it from the machine. 16. Transfer the ice cream into serving bowls and serve immediately.

Serving Suggestions: Serve in sugared cones.
Variation Tip: Use organic food coloring.
Nutritional Information per Serving: Calories: 196 |Fat: 13.1g|Sat Fat: 8.1g|Carbohydrates: 18.6g|Fiber: 0g|Sugar: 18.2g|Protein: 2.6g

Chapter 4 Ice Creams Mix-Ins

Pistachio Ice Cream 39

Blueberry Graham Crackers Ice Cream 39

Strawberry-Chocolate Ice Cream 40

Cheesy Cherry Ice Cream 40

Brown Sugar Walnut Ice Cream 41

Homemade Caramel Chocolate Chips Ice Cream 41

Vanilla White Chocolate Ice Cream 42

Easy Chocolate Banana Pudding Ice Cream 42

Caramel Protein and Green M&M Ice Cream 43

Pistachio Banana Ice Cream 43

Raspberry Cottage Cheese Ice Cream 44

Sweet Chocolate Chips Ice Cream 44

Tasty Chocolate Sandwich Cookies Ice Cream 45

Fresh Strawberry & Banana Cookies Ice Cream 45

Vanilla Pudding Almond Ice Cream 46

Simple Vanilla Pecan Ice Cream 46

Pistachio Ice Cream

⏱ Prep: 10 minutes   🍳 Cook: 10 seconds   🍽 Serves: 4

Ingredients:

1 tablespoon cream cheese
⅓ cup granulated sugar
1 teaspoon almond extract
¾ cup heavy cream
1 cup whole milk
¼ cup pistachios, chopped

Preparation:

1. In a large-sized, microwave-safe bowl, put in cream cheese and microwave for 10 seconds. 2. Put in sugar and almond extract and whisk to form a frosting mixture. 3. Slowly put in the heavy cream and milk and whisk to incorporate thoroughly. 4. Transfer the blended mixture into an empty Ninja CREAMi pint container. 5. Cover the container with the storage lid and freeze for 24 hours. 6. After 24 hours, take off the lid from container and arrange into the outer bowl of Ninja CREAMi. 7. Install the "Creamerizer Paddle" onto the lid of outer bowl. 8. Then rotate the lid clockwise to lock. 9. Press "Power" button to turn on the unit. 10. Then press "ICE CREAM" button. 11. When the program is completed, with a spoon, create a 1½-inch wide hole in the center that reaches the bottom of the pint container. 12. Add pistachios in the hole and press "MIX-IN" button. 13. When the program is completed, turn the outer bowl and release it from the machine. 14. Transfer the ice cream into serving bowls and enjoy immediately.

Serving Suggestions: This ice cream will go greatly with fruit crumbles.
Variation Tip: Use full-fat cream cheese.
Nutritional Information per Serving: Calories: 259 |Fat: 15.2g|Sat Fat: 9.9g|Carbohydrates: 29.3g|Fiber: 0g|Sugar: 29g|Protein: 2.6g

Blueberry Graham Crackers Ice Cream

⏱ Prep: 15 minutes   🍽 Serves: 4

Ingredients:

½ cup frozen blueberries, thawed and squeezed
½ cup brown sugar
1 cup whole milk
½ teaspoon almond extract
½ teaspoon vanilla extract
⅓ cup heavy cream
⅓ cup graham crackers, crushed

Preparation:

1. In a high-powered blender, put in blueberries and remaining ingredients except for chocolate chips and process to form a smooth mixture. 2. Transfer the blended mixture into an empty Ninja CREAMi pint container. 3. Put in heavy cream and blend to incorporate. 4. Cover the container with the storage lid and freeze for 24 hours. 5. After 24 hours, take off the lid from container and arrange into the outer bowl of Ninja CREAMi. 6. Install the "Creamerizer Paddle" onto the lid of outer bowl. 7. Then rotate the lid clockwise to lock. 8. Press "Power" button to turn on the unit. 9. Then press "ICE CREAM" button. 10. When the program is completed, with a spoon, create a 1½-inch wide hole in the center that reaches the bottom of the pint container. 11. Add graham crackers in the hole and press "MIX-IN" button. 12. When the program is completed, turn the outer bowl and release it from the machine. 13. Transfer the ice cream into serving bowls and enjoy immediately.

Serving Suggestions: Serve with a garnishing of chocolate chips.
Variation Tip: You can use more vanilla extract instead of almond extract.
Nutritional Information per Serving: Calories: 250 |Fat: 9.9g|Sat Fat: 6.4g|Carbohydrates: 38.6g|Fiber: 0.8g|Sugar: 37.3g|Protein: 3.4g

Strawberry-Chocolate Ice Cream

⏰ Prep: 10 minute   📚 Serves: 4

Ingredients:

1 cup strawberry milk
½ cup strawberry yogurt
¼ cup coffee creamer
½ teaspoon vanilla extract
1 tablespoon whipping cream
3 teaspoons mini chocolate chips

Preparation:

1. In an empty Ninja CREAMi pint container, put in milk, yogurt, creamer, vanilla extract and whipping cream and blend to incorporate. 2. Cover the container with storage lid and freeze for 24 hours. 3. After 24 hours, take off the lid from container and arrange into the outer bowl of Ninja CREAMi. 4. Install the "Creamerizer Paddle" onto the lid of outer bowl. 5. Then rotate the lid clockwise to lock. 6. Press "Power" button to turn on the unit. 7. Then press "ICE CREAM" button. 8. When the program is completed, with a spoon, create a 1½-inch wide hole in the center that reaches the bottom of the pint container. 9. Put in pecans and chocolate chips in the hole and press "MIX-IN" button. 10. When the program is completed, turn the outer bowl and release it from the machine. 11. Transfer the ice cream into serving bowls and enjoy immediately.

Serving Suggestions: Serve in a fancy glass bowl.
Variation Tip: Use full-fat yogurt.
Nutritional Information per Serving: Calories: 103 |Fat: 4.1g|Sat Fat: 2.9g|Carbohydrates: 8.1g|Fiber: 0.1g|Sugar: 8.3g|Protein: 5.1g

Cheesy Cherry Ice Cream

⏰ Prep: 10 minutes   🍳 Cook: 5 minutes   📚 Serves: 4

Ingredients:

1 cup heavy cream
½ cup whole milk
¼ cup maple syrup
2 ounces mascarpone cheese
2 tablespoons cherry jam
2 tablespoons lemon curd
¼ cup cherries, pitted and chopped

Preparation:

1. In a small-sized saucepan, put cream, milk, and maple syrup on burner at around medium heat and cook until heated through, stirring continuously. 2. Add in the mascarpone cheese and stir to incorporate thoroughly. 3. Transfer the blended mixture into an empty Ninja CREAMi pint container. 4. Place the container into an ice bath to cool. 5. After cooling, cover the container with the storage lid and freeze for 24 hours. 6. After 24 hours, take off the lid from container and arrange into the outer bowl of Ninja CREAMi. 7. Install the "Creamerizer Paddle" onto the lid of outer bowl. 8. Then rotate the lid clockwise to lock. 9. Press "Power" button to turn on the unit. 10. Then press "ICE CREAM" button. 11. When the program is completed, with a spoon, create a 1½-inch wide hole in the center that reaches the bottom of the pint container. 12. Add the jam, lemon curd and cherries in the hole and press "MIX-IN" button. 13. When the program is completed, turn the outer bowl and release it from the machine. 14. Transfer the ice cream into serving bowls and enjoy immediately.

Serving Suggestions: Serve with a topping of fresh fruit.
Variation Tip: Feel free to use jam of your choice.
Nutritional Information per Serving: Calories: 351 |Fat: 23.3g|Sat Fat: 12.1g|Carbohydrates: 32.8g|Fiber: 1.8g|Sugar: 28.6g|Protein: 7.9g

Brown Sugar Walnut Ice Cream

⏱ **Prep: 10 minutes** 🍳 **Cook: 10 seconds** 🍽 **Serves: 4**

Ingredients:

1 tablespoon cream cheese
⅓ cup brown sugar
1 teaspoon vanilla extract
¾ cup heavy cream
1 cup whole milk
¼ cup walnuts, chopped

Preparation:

1. In a large-sized, microwave-safe bowl, put in cream cheese and microwave for 10 seconds. 2. Put in brown sugar and vanilla extract and whisk to form a frosting mixture. 3. Slowly put in the heavy cream and milk and whisk to incorporate thoroughly. 4. Transfer the blended mixture into an empty Ninja CREAMi pint container. 5. Cover the container with the storage lid and freeze for 24 hours. 6. After 24 hours, take off the lid from container and arrange into the outer bowl of Ninja CREAMi. 7. Install the "Creamerizer Paddle" onto the lid of outer bowl. 8. Then rotate the lid clockwise to lock. 9. Press "Power" button to turn on the unit. 10. Then press "ICE CREAM" button. 11. When the program is completed, with a spoon, create a 1½-inch wide hole in the center that reaches the bottom of the pint container. 12. Add walnuts in the hole and press "MIX-IN" button. 13. When the program is completed, turn the outer bowl and release it from the machine. 14. Transfer the ice cream into serving bowls and enjoy immediately.

Serving Suggestions: Serve in a sugary cone.
Variation Tip: Make sure to use unsalted walnuts.
Nutritional Information per Serving: Calories: 245 |Fat: 14.3g|Sat Fat: 9.1g|Carbohydrates: 26.5g|Fiber: 0.4g|Sugar: 25.5g|Protein: 3.4g

Homemade Caramel Chocolate Chips Ice Cream

⏱ **Prep: 10 minutes** 🍽 **Serves: 4**

Ingredients:

1 (11½ ounce) bottle caramel protein shake
⅓ cup chocolate chips

Preparation:

1. In an empty Ninja CREAMi pint container, put the protein shake. 2. Cover the container with storage lid and freeze for 24 hours. 3. After 24 hours, take off the lid from container and arrange into the outer bowl of Ninja CREAMi. 4. Install the "Creamerizer Paddle" onto the lid of outer bowl. 5. Then rotate the lid clockwise to lock. 6. Press "Power" button to turn on the unit. 7. Then press "ICE CREAM" button. 8. When the program is completed, with a spoon, create a 1½-inch wide hole in the center that reaches the bottom of the pint container. 9. Add the chocolate chips in the hole and press "MIX-IN" button. 10. When the program is completed, turn the outer bowl and release it from the machine. 11. Transfer the ice cream into serving bowls and enjoy immediately.

Serving Suggestions: Serve with a topping of chocolate chips.
Variation Tip: You can use shake of choice.
Nutritional Information per Serving: Calories: 389 |Fat: 6g|Sat Fat: 2.1g|Carbohydrates: 54g|Fiber: 0.8g|Sugar: 42g|Protein: 33.5g

Vanilla White Chocolate Ice Cream

⏰ **Prep: 10 minutes**   🍳 **Cook: 10 seconds**   🍽 **Serves: 4**

Ingredients:

1 tablespoon cream cheese
⅓ cup granulated sugar
1 teaspoon vanilla extract
¾ cup heavy cream
1 cup whole milk
¼ cup white chocolate bar, finely cut up

Preparation:

1. In a large-sized, microwave-safe bowl, put in cream cheese and microwave for 10 seconds. 2. Put in sugar and vanilla extract and whisk to form a frosting mixture. 3. Slowly put in the heavy cream and milk and whisk to incorporate thoroughly. 4. Transfer the blended mixture into an empty Ninja CREAMi pint container. 5. Cover the container with the storage lid and freeze for 24 hours. 6. After 24 hours, take off the lid from container and arrange into the outer bowl of Ninja CREAMi. 7. Install the "Creamerizer Paddle" onto the lid of outer bowl. 8. Then rotate the lid clockwise to lock. 9. Press "Power" button to turn on the unit. 10. Then press "ICE CREAM" button. 11. When the program is completed, with a spoon, create a 1½-inch wide hole in the center that reaches the bottom of the pint container. 12. Add chocolate pieces in the hole and press "MIX-IN" button. 13. When the program is completed, turn the outer bowl and release it from the machine. 14. Transfer the ice cream into serving bowls and enjoy immediately.

Serving Suggestions: Serve with a topping of berries.
Variation Tip: Make sure to use best quality chocolate.
Nutritional Information per Serving: Calories: 246 |Fat: 14.1g|Sat Fat: 9.3g|Carbohydrates: 26.6g|Fiber: 0.3g|Sugar: 25.2g|Protein: 3.5g

Easy Chocolate Banana Pudding Ice Cream

⏰ **Prep: 10 minutes**   🍽 **Serves: 4**

Ingredients:

1 (3.4-ounce) box instant banana pudding mix
1½ cups whole milk
½ cup heavy whipping cream
¼ cup mini chocolate chips

Preparation:

1. In a large-sized bowl, put pudding mix, milk and whipping cream and whisk to incorporate thoroughly. 2. Transfer the blended mixture into an empty Ninja CREAMi pint container. 3. Cover the container with storage lid and freeze for 24 hours. 4. After 24 hours, take off the lid from container and arrange into the outer bowl of Ninja CREAMi. 5. Install the "Creamerizer Paddle" onto the lid of outer bowl. 6. Then rotate the lid clockwise to lock. 7. Press "Power" button to turn on the unit. 8. Then press "ICE CREAM" button. 9. When the program is completed, with a spoon, create a 1½-inch wide hole in the center that reaches the bottom of the pint container. 10. Add the chocolate chips in the hole and press "MIX-IN" button. 11. When the program is completed, turn the outer bowl and release it from the machine. 12. Transfer the ice cream into serving bowls and enjoy immediately.

Serving Suggestions: Serve with a topping of chopped nuts.
Variation Tip: Use semi-sweet chocolate chips.
Nutritional Information per Serving: Calories: 213 |Fat: 10.3g|Sat Fat: 5.4g|Carbohydrates: 26.8g||Fiber: 1.4g|Sugar: 19.2g|Protein: 4.21g

Caramel Protein and Green M&M Ice Cream

⏰ **Prep: 10 minutes** 🍥 **Serves: 4**

🟢 **Ingredients:**

1 (11½-ounce) bottle caramel protein shake
⅓ cup green M&M

🟢 **Preparation:**

1. In an empty Ninja CREAMi pint container, put in protein shake. 2. Cover the container with storage lid and freeze for 24 hours. 3. After 24 hours, take off the lid from container and arrange into the outer bowl of Ninja CREAMi. 4. Install the "Creamerizer Paddle" onto the lid of outer bowl. 5. Then rotate the lid clockwise to lock. 6. Press "Power" button to turn on the unit. 7. Then press "ICE CREAM" button. 8. When the program is completed, with a spoon, create a 1½-inch wide hole in the center that reaches the bottom of the pint container. 9. Add the M&M in the hole and press "MIX-IN" button. 10. When the program is completed, turn the outer bowl and release it from the machine. 11. Transfer the ice cream into serving bowls and enjoy immediately.

Serving Suggestions: Serve with a topping of extra M&Ms.
Variation Tip: Feel free to use M&Ms of your choice.
Nutritional Information per Serving: Calories: 110 |Fat: 4.4g|Sat Fat: 1.8g|Carbohydrates: 12.6g|Fiber: 0.8g|Sugar:10.3g|Protein: 5g

Pistachio Banana Ice Cream

⏰ **Prep: 10 minutes** 🍥 **Serves: 4**

🟢 **Ingredients:**

1 (11.5-ounce) bottle vanilla protein shake
1 small banana, peel removed
1 tablespoon pistachios, cut up

🟢 **Preparation:**

1. In a high-powered blender, put in protein shake and banana and process to form a smooth mixture. 2. Transfer the blended mixture into an empty Ninja CREAMi pint container. 3. Cover the container with the storage lid and freeze for 24 hours. 4. After 24 hours, take off the lid from container and arrange into the outer bowl of Ninja CREAMi. 5. Install the "Creamerizer Paddle" onto the lid of outer bowl. 6. Then rotate the lid clockwise to lock. 7. Press "Power" button to turn on the unit. 8. Then press "LITE ICE CREAM" button. 9. When the program is completed, with a spoon, create a 1½-inch wide hole in the center that reaches the bottom of the pint container. 10. Add pistachios in the hole and press "MIX-IN" button. 11. When the program is completed, turn the outer bowl and release it from the machine. 12. Transfer the ice cream into serving bowls and enjoy immediately.

Serving Suggestions: Serve with a garnishing of pistachios.
Variation Tip: You can use shake of your choice.
Nutritional Information per Serving: Calories: 330 |Fat: 2.9g|Sat Fat: 0.1g|Carbohydrates: 45.6g|Fiber: 0.8g|Sugar:33.4g|Protein: 33.1g

Raspberry Cottage Cheese Ice Cream

⏰ **Prep: 10 minutes**   📚 **Serves: 4**

Ingredients:

1 (11.5 ounce) bottle vanilla protein shake
½ cup cottage cheese
¼ teaspoon vanilla extract
½ cup fresh raspberries, cut up
½ graham cracker, broken into pieces

Preparation:

1. In a high-powered blender, put in protein shake, cottage cheese, and vanilla extract and process to form a smooth mixture. 2. Transfer the blended mixture into an empty Ninja CREAMi pint container. 3. Cover the container with the storage lid and freeze for 24 hours. 4. After 24 hours, take off the lid from container and arrange into the outer bowl of Ninja CREAMi. 5. Install the "Creamerizer Paddle" onto the lid of outer bowl. 6. Then rotate the lid clockwise to lock. 7. Press "Power" button to turn on the unit. 8. Then press "ICE CREAM" button. 9. When the program is completed, with a spoon, create a 1½-inch wide hole in the center that reaches the bottom of the pint container. 10. Add raspberries and graham cracker in the hole and press "MIX-IN" button. 11. When the program is completed, turn the outer bowl and release it from the machine. 12. Transfer the ice cream into serving bowls and enjoy immediately.

Serving Suggestions: Serve with a topping of berry sauce.
Variation Tip: Look for fully red and ripe raspberries.
Nutritional Information per Serving: Calories: 344 |Fat: 3.2g|Sat Fat: 0.4g|Carbohydrates: 43.9g|Fiber: 1.1g|Sugar: 31.6g|Protein: 36.8g

Sweet Chocolate Chips Ice Cream

⏰ **Prep: 10 minutes**   🍳 **Cook: 10 seconds**   📚 **Serves: 4**

Ingredients:

1 tablespoon cream cheese
⅓ cup sugar
1 teaspoon vanilla extract
1 cup whole milk
¾ cup heavy cream
¼ cup mini chocolate chips

Preparation:

1. In a large-sized, microwave-safe bowl, put in cream cheese and microwave for 10 seconds. 2. Put in sugar and vanilla extract and whisk to form a frosting mixture. 3. Slowly put in heavy cream and milk and whisk to incorporate thoroughly. 4. Transfer the blended mixture into an empty Ninja CREAMi pint container. 5. Cover the container with the storage lid and freeze for 24 hours. 6. After 24 hours, take off the lid from container and arrange into the outer bowl of Ninja CREAMi. 7. Install the "Creamerizer Paddle" onto the lid of outer bowl. 8. Then rotate the lid clockwise to lock. 9. Press "Power" button to turn on the unit. 10. Then press "ICE CREAM" button. 11. When the program is completed, with a spoon, create a 1½-inch wide hole in the center that reaches the bottom of the pint container. 12. Add chocolate chips in the hole and press "MIX-IN" button. 13. When the program is completed, turn the outer bowl and release it from the machine. 14. Transfer the ice cream into serving bowls and enjoy immediately.

Serving Suggestions: Serve with a drizzling of chocolate sauce.
Variation Tip: Use semi-sweet chocolate chips.
Nutritional Information per Serving: Calories: 245 |Fat: 14.3g|Sat Fat: 9.1g|Carbohydrates: 26.5g|Fiber: 0.4g|Sugar: 25.5g|Protein: 3.4g

Tasty Chocolate Sandwich Cookies Ice Cream

⏰ Prep: 10 minutes   🍴 Serves: 4

Ingredients:

1 cup whole milk
½ cup white sugar
2 tablespoons cream cheese
¼ teaspoon ground cinnamon
¼ cup chocolate sandwich cookies, crumbled

Preparation:

1. In a high-powered blender, put in milk, brown sugar, cream cheese and cinnamon and process to form a smooth mixture. 2. Transfer the blended mixture into an empty Ninja CREAMi pint container. 3. Cover the container with the storage lid and freeze for 24 hours. 4. After 24 hours, take off the lid from container and arrange into the outer bowl of Ninja CREAMi. 5. Install the "Creamerizer Paddle" onto the lid of outer bowl. 6. Then rotate the lid clockwise to lock. 7. Press "Power" button to turn on the unit. 8. Then press "ICE CREAM" button. 9. When the program is completed, with a spoon, create a 1½-inch wide hole in the center that reaches the bottom of the pint container. 10. Add cookies in the hole and press "MIX-IN" button. 11. When the program is completed, turn the outer bowl and release it from the machine. 12. Transfer the ice cream into serving bowls and enjoy immediately.
Serving Suggestions: Serve with a sprinkling of cocoa powder.
Variation Tip: Use high-quality cookies.
Nutritional Information per Serving: Calories: 268 |Fat: 8.2g|Sat Fat: 3.4g|Carbohydrates: 8.2g|Fiber: 46.8g|Sugar: 38.7g|Protein: 3.9g

Fresh Strawberry & Banana Cookies Ice Cream

Prep: 10 minutes   🍴 Serves: 4

Ingredients:

⅔ cup heavy cream
¼ cup honey
1 tablespoon sour cream
½ tablespoon fresh lime juice
½ tablespoon vanilla extract
6 ounces fresh strawberries, hulled and sliced
1 small banana, peel removed and sliced
¼ cup oatmeal cookies, crumbled

Preparation:

1. In a large-sized bowl, put in heavy cream, honey, sour cream, fresh lime juice and vanilla extract and with a wire whisk, whisk until the mixture looks like frosting. 2. Add the strawberry and banana slices and blend to incorporate. 3. Transfer the blended mixture into an empty Ninja CREAMi pint container. 4. Place the container into an ice bath to cool. 5. After cooling, cover the container with the storage lid and freeze for 24 hours. 6. After 24 hours, take off the lid from container and arrange into the outer bowl of Ninja CREAMi. 7. Install the "Creamerizer Paddle" onto the lid of outer bowl. 8. Then rotate the lid clockwise to lock. 9. Press "Power" button to turn on the unit. 10. Then press "ICE CREAM" button. 11. When the program is completed, with a spoon, create a 1½-inch wide hole in the center that reaches the bottom of the pint container. 12. Add the crumbled cookies in the hole and press "MIX-IN" button. 13. When the program is completed, turn the outer bowl and release it from the machine. 14. Transfer the ice cream into serving bowls and enjoy immediately.
Serving Suggestions: Serve with a topping of fresh strawberries.
Variation Tip: Don't use overripe strawberries.
Nutritional Information per Serving: Calories: 206 |Fat: 9.1g|Sat Fat: 5.3g|Carbohydrates: 31.4g|Fiber: 1.7g|Sugar: 24.8g|Protein: 1.4g

Vanilla Pudding Almond Ice Cream

⏱ **Prep: 10 minutes**   📚 **Serves: 4**

Ingredients:

1 (3.4-ounce) box instant vanilla pudding mix
1½ cups whole milk
½ cup heavy whipping cream
¼ cup almonds, cut up

Preparation:

1. In a large-sized bowl, put in pudding mix, milk and whipping cream and whisk to incorporate thoroughly. 2. Transfer the blended mixture into an empty Ninja CREAMi pint container. 3. Cover the container with storage lid and freeze for 24 hours. 4. After 24 hours, take off the lid from container and arrange into the outer bowl of Ninja CREAMi. 5. Install the "Creamerizer Paddle" onto the lid of outer bowl. 6. Then rotate the lid clockwise to lock. 7. Press "Power" button to turn on the unit. 8. Then press "ICE CREAM" button. 9. When the program is completed, with a spoon, create a 1½-inch wide hole in the center that reaches the bottom of the pint container. 10. Add the almonds in the hole and press "MIX-IN" button. 11. When the program is completed, turn the outer bowl and release it from the machine. 12. Transfer the ice cream into serving bowls and enjoy immediately.

Serving Suggestions: Serve with a drizzling of caramel sauce.
Variation Tip: You can use banana pudding in this recipe.
Nutritional Information per Serving: Calories: 168 |Fat: 12.2g|Sat Fat: 5.8g|Carbohydrates: 10.6g|Fiber: 0.7g|Sugar: 9.4g|Protein: 5.2g

Simple Vanilla Pecan Ice Cream

⏱ **Prep: 10 minutes**   🍳 **Cook: 10 seconds**   📚 **Serves: 4**

Ingredients:

1 tablespoon cream cheese
⅓ cup granulated sugar
1 teaspoon vanilla extract
¾ cup heavy cream
1 cup whole milk
¼ cup pecans, cut up

Preparation:

1. In a large-sized, microwave-safe bowl, put in cream cheese and microwave for 10 seconds. 2. Put in sugar and vanilla extract and whisk to form a frosting mixture. 3. Slowly put in heavy cream and milk and whisk to incorporate thoroughly. 4. Transfer the blended mixture into an empty Ninja CREAMi pint container. 5. Cover the container with the storage lid and freeze for 24 hours. 6. After 24 hours, take off the lid from container and arrange into the outer bowl of Ninja CREAMi. 7. Install the "Creamerizer Paddle" onto the lid of outer bowl. 8. Then rotate the lid clockwise to lock. 9. Press "Power" button to turn on the unit. 10. Then press "ICE CREAM" button. 11. When the program is completed, with a spoon, create a 1½-inch wide hole in the center that reaches the bottom of the pint container. 12. Add pecans in the hole and press "MIX-IN" button. 13. When the program is completed, turn the outer bowl and release it from the machine. 14. Transfer the ice cream into serving bowls and enjoy immediately.

Serving Suggestions: Serve with a topping of extra nuts.
Variation Tip: Walnuts can be replaced with pecans.
Nutritional Information per Serving: Calories: 248 |Fat: 17.3g|Sat Fat: 7.5g|Carbohydrates: 21.5g|Fiber: 0.9g|Sugar: 20.3g|Protein: 3.5g

Chapter 5 Sorbets

Sorbets ……………………………………………………………………	47
Citrus Pineapple Margarita Sorbet…………………………………	48
Super-Easy Orange Sorbet ………………………………………………	48
Simple Mango Sorbet …………………………………………………	49
Fresh Peach Sorbet ……………………………………………………	49
Sweet Cherry Sorbet……………………………………………………	50
Yummy Ginger Beer Blueberry Sorbet …………………………………	50
Limey Raspberry Sorbet ………………………………………………	51
Refreshing Strawberry Sorbet…………………………………………	51
Light Kiwi Banana Sorbet ……………………………………………	52
Citrus Mango Sorbet …………………………………………………	52
Gingered Pumpkin Puree Sorbet………………………………………	53
Maple Peach Liqueur Sorbet …………………………………………	53
Zesty Cherry Sorbet ……………………………………………………	54
Mixed Berries and Orange Sorbet ……………………………………	54
Quick Orange Beer Sorbet ……………………………………………	55
Tasty Strawberry Ginger Ale Sorbet …………………………………	55
Lemony Plum Sorbet …………………………………………………	56

Citrus Pineapple Margarita Sorbet

⏰ Prep: 10 minutes 📚 Serves: 4

Ingredients:

¾ cup margarita mix
3 tablespoons light rum
2 tablespoons fresh orange juice
1 tablespoon honey
1 (15-ounce) can pineapple chunks

Preparation:

1. In a bowl, put margarita mix and remaining ingredients except for pineapple chunks and whisk to incorporate thoroughly. 2. Add pineapple chunks and toss to coat. 3. Transfer the blended mixture into an empty Ninja CREAMi pint container. 4. Cover the container with storage lid and freeze for 24 hours. 5. After 24 hours, take off the lid from container and arrange into the outer bowl of Ninja CREAMi. 6. Install the "Creamerizer Paddle" onto the lid of outer bowl. 7. Then rotate the lid clockwise to lock. 8. Press "Power" button to turn on the unit. 9. Then press "SORBET" button. 10. When the program is completed, turn the outer bowl and release it from the machine. 11. Transfer the sorbet into serving bowls and enjoy immediately.

Serving Suggestions: Serve alongside fresh pineapple slices.
Variation Tip: Gold tequila can be used instead of rum.
Nutritional Information per Serving: Calories: 132 |Fat: 0.4g|Sat Fat: 0g|Carbohydrates: 27g|Fiber: 2g|Sugar: 24.3g|Protein: 0.9g

Super-Easy Orange Sorbet

⏰ Prep: 10 minutes 📚 Serves: 4

Ingredients:

1 cup warm water
½ cup fresh orange juice
½ cup white sugar
1 tablespoon honey

Preparation:

1. In a large-sized bowl, put water and remaining ingredients and whisk to incorporate thoroughly. 2. Transfer the blended mixture into an empty Ninja CREAMi pint container. 3. Cover the container with storage lid and freeze for 24 hours. 4. After 24 hours, take off the lid from container and arrange into the outer bowl of Ninja CREAMi. 5. Install the "Creamerizer Paddle" onto the lid of outer bowl. 6. Then rotate the lid clockwise to lock. 7. Press "Power" button to turn on the unit. 8. Then press "SORBET" button. 9. When the program is completed, turn the outer bowl and release it from the machine. 10. Transfer the sorbet into serving bowls and enjoy immediately.

Serving Suggestions: Serve with a topping of lime zest.
Variation Tip: Make sure to use warm water.
Nutritional Information per Serving: Calories: 120 |Fat: 0.2g|Sat Fat: 0.1g|Carbohydrates: 36g|Fiber: 0.9g|Sugar: 32.1g|Protein: 0.5g

Simple Mango Sorbet

⏰ **Prep: 10 minutes**   📚 **Serves: 4**

Ingredients:
1 (15-ounce) can mango chunks in light syrup

Preparation:
1. Place the mango pieces into an empty Ninja CREAMi container to the MAX FILL line. 2. Cover the mango pieces with syrup from the can. 3. Transfer the blended mixture into an empty Ninja CREAMi pint container. 4. Cover the container with storage lid and freeze for 24 hours. 5. After 24 hours, take off the lid from container and arrange into the outer bowl of Ninja CREAMi. 6. Install the "Creamerizer Paddle" onto the lid of outer bowl. 7. Then rotate the lid clockwise to lock. 8. Press "Power" button to turn on the unit. 9. Then press "SORBET" button. 10. When the program is completed, turn the outer bowl and release it from the machine. 11. Transfer the sorbet into serving bowls and enjoy immediately.

Serving Suggestions: Serve alongside fresh mango chunks.
Variation Tip: You can use fruit of your choice.
Nutritional Information per Serving: Calories: 221 |Fat: 1.5g|Sat Fat: 0g|Carbohydrates: 52.5g|Fiber: 8.6g|Sugar: 52.5g|Protein: 5.3g

Fresh Peach Sorbet

⏰ **Prep: 10 minutes**   📚 **Serves: 4**

Ingredients:
2 cups fresh peach puree
¼ cup brown sugar
1 tablespoon full-fat coconut milk

Preparation:
1. In a medium-sized bowl, put peach puree, brown sugar and coconut milk and whisk to incorporate thoroughly. 2. Transfer the blended mixture into an empty Ninja CREAMi pint container. 3. Cover the container with storage lid and freeze for 24 hours. 4. After 24 hours, take off the lid from container and arrange into the outer bowl of Ninja CREAMi. 5. Install the "Creamerizer Paddle" onto the lid of outer bowl. 6. Then rotate the lid clockwise to lock. 7. Press "Power" button to turn on the unit. 8. Then press "SORBET" button. 9. When the program is completed, turn the outer bowl and release it from the machine. 10. Transfer the sorbet into serving bowls and enjoy immediately.

Serving Suggestions: Serve with a topping of crystallized ginger.
Variation Tip: For the best result, use a freshly blended puree of peach.
Nutritional Information per Serving: Calories: 361 |Fat: 0.2g|Sat Fat: 0.1g|Carbohydrates: 90.6g|Fiber: 5.8g|Sugar: 73.8g|Protein: 2.1g

Sweet Cherry Sorbet

⏰ **Prep: 10 minutes** ≋ **Serves: 4**

> **Ingredients:**

3 cups fresh cherries, pitted and halved
3-4 drops liquid stevia

> **Preparation:**

1. In an empty Ninja CREAMi pint container, put the cherries and stevia and with a potato masher, mash thoroughly. 2. Cover the container with storage lid and freeze for 24 hours. 3. After 24 hours, take off the lid from container and arrange into the outer bowl of Ninja CREAMi. 4. Install the "Creamerizer Paddle" onto the lid of outer bowl. 5. Then rotate the lid clockwise to lock. 6. Press "Power" button to turn on the unit. 7. Then press "SORBET" button. 8. When the program is completed, turn the outer bowl and release it from the machine. 9. Transfer the sorbet into serving bowls and serve immediately.

Serving Suggestions: Serve with a topping of whipped cream.
Variation Tip: Use fresh sweet cherries.
Nutritional Information per Serving: Calories: 68 |Fat: 0g|Sat Fat: 0g|Carbohydrates: 16.6g|Fiber: 2.3g|Sugar: 14.3g|Protein: 1.5g

Yummy Ginger Beer Blueberry Sorbet

⏰ **Prep: 10 minutes** ≋ **Serves: 4**

> **Ingredients:**

3 cups fresh blueberries
⅓ cup water
⅓ cup brown sugar
¾ cup ginger beer

> **Preparation:**

1. In a high-speed blender, put in blueberries and remaining ingredients and process to form a smooth mixture. 2. Transfer the blended mixture into an empty Ninja CREAMi pint container. 3. Cover the container with storage lid and freeze for 24 hours. 4. After 24 hours, take off the lid from container and arrange into the outer bowl of Ninja CREAMi. 5. Install the "Creamerizer Paddle" onto the lid of outer bowl. 6. Then rotate the lid clockwise to lock. 7. Press "Power" button to turn on the unit. 8. Then press "SORBET" button. 9. When the program is completed, turn the outer bowl and release it from the machine. 10. Transfer the sorbet into serving bowls and enjoy immediately.

Serving Suggestions: Serve
Variation Tip: You can replace ginger beer with ginger ale.
Nutritional Information per Serving: Calories: 113 |Fat: 0.3g|Sat Fat: 0g|Carbohydrates: 29g|Fiber: 2.2g|Sugar: 25.9g|Protein: 0.7g

Limey Raspberry Sorbet

⏲ Prep: 10 minutes   ≋ Serves: 4

Ingredients:

1 pound frozen raspberries
4¼ ounces granulated sugar
1 teaspoon fresh lime juice

Preparation:

1. In a high-powered blender, put in raspberries and remaining ingredients and process to form a smooth mixture. 2. Transfer the blended mixture into an empty Ninja CREAMi pint container. 3. Cover the container with storage lid and freeze for 24 hours. 4. After 24 hours, take off the lid from container and arrange into the outer bowl of Ninja CREAMi. 5. Install the "Creamerizer Paddle" onto the lid of outer bowl. 6. Then rotate the lid clockwise to lock. 7. Press "Power" button to turn on the unit. 8. Then press "SORBET" button. 9. When the program is completed, turn the outer bowl and release it from the machine. 10. Transfer the sorbet into serving bowls and enjoy immediately.

Serving Suggestions: Serve this ice cream alongside fresh fruit.
Variation Tip: Feel free to use berries of your choice.
Nutritional Information per Serving: Calories: 178 |Fat: 0.4g|Sat Fat: 0g|Carbohydrates: 44g|Fiber: 4.1g|Sugar: 38.2g|Protein: 0.8g

Refreshing Strawberry Sorbet

⏲ Prep: 10 minutes   ≋ Serves: 4

Ingredients:

¾ cup frozen strawberry juice concentrate
1½ cups water
1 tablespoon fresh lime juice

Preparation:

1. In a bowl, put juice concentrate and remaining ingredients and beat to incorporate thoroughly. 2. Transfer the mixture into an empty Ninja CREAMi pint container. 3. Cover the container with storage lid and freeze for 24 hours. 4. After 24 hours, take off the lid from container and arrange into the outer bowl of Ninja CREAMi. 5. Install the "Creamerizer Paddle" onto the lid of outer bowl. 6. Then rotate the lid clockwise to lock. 7. Press "Power" button to turn on the unit. 8. Then press "SORBET" button. 9. When the program is completed, turn the outer bowl and release it from the machine. 10. Transfer the sorbet into serving bowls and serve immediately.

Serving Suggestions: Serve with a garnishing of lime zest.
Variation Tip: Use Freshly squeezed lime juice.
Nutritional Information per Serving: Calories: 23 | Fat: 0.1g|Sat Fat: 0g|Carbohydrates: 5.1g|Fiber: 0.1g|Sugar: 5.9g|Protein: 0.2g

Light Kiwi Banana Sorbet

⏰ **Prep:** 10 minutes 📚 **Serves:** 4

Ingredients:

2 cups frozen bananas, sliced
4 kiwis, peeled and cut into 1-inch pieces
¼ cup maple syrup
¼ cup water

Preparation:

1. In a high-speed blender, put bananas and remaining ingredients and process to form a smooth mixture. 2. Transfer the mixture into an empty Ninja CREAMi pint container. 3. Cover the container with storage lid and freeze for 24 hours. 4. After 24 hours, take off the lid from container and arrange into the outer bowl of Ninja CREAMi. 5. Install the "Creamerizer Paddle" onto the lid of outer bowl. 6. Then rotate the lid clockwise to lock. 7. Press "Power" button to turn on the unit. 8. Then press "SORBET" button. 9. When the program is completed, turn the outer bowl and release it from the machine. 10. Transfer the sorbet into serving bowls and serve immediately.

Serving Suggestions: Serve with the garnishing of shredded coconut.
Variation Tip: You can use sweetener of your choice.
Nutritional Information per Serving: Calories: 131 | Fat: 0.4g|Sat Fat: 0g|Carbohydrates: 33.7g|Fiber: 4.8g|Sugar: 26.3g|Protein: 0.9g

Citrus Mango Sorbet

⏰ **Prep:** 10 minutes 📚 **Serves:** 4

Ingredients:

1 cup fresh mango, peel removed, pitted and sliced
¼ cup orange juice

Preparation:

1. In a high-powered blender, put in mango slices and orange juice and process to form a smooth mixture. 2. Transfer the blended mixture into an empty Ninja CREAMi pint container. 3. Cover the container with storage lid and freeze for 24 hours. 4. After 24 hours, take off the lid from container and arrange into the outer bowl of Ninja CREAMi. 5. Install the "Creamerizer Paddle" onto the lid of outer bowl. 6. Then rotate the lid clockwise to lock. 7. Press "Power" button to turn on the unit. 8. Then press "SORBET" button. 9. When the program is completed, turn the outer bowl and release it from the machine. 10. Transfer the sorbet into serving bowls and enjoy immediately.

Serving Suggestions: Serve with a topping of coconut flakes.
Variation Tip: Use sweetened mango.
Nutritional Information per Serving: Calories: 32 |Fat: 0.2g|Sat Fat: 0.1g|Carbohydrates: 7.8g|Fiber: 0.7g|Sugar: 6.9g|Protein: 0.5g

Gingered Pumpkin Puree Sorbet

⏱ **Prep: 10 minutes**   ◈ **Serves: 4**

Ingredients:

2½ cups pumpkin puree
½ cup brown sugar
2 teaspoons fresh orange juice
½ cup coconut water
2 tablespoons fresh ginger, peel removed and finely cut up

Preparation:

1. In a large-sized owl, put in pumpkin puree, brown sugar, orange juice, coconut water and ginger and mix until blended thoroughly. 2. Transfer the blended mixture into an empty Ninja CREAMi pint container. 3. Cover the container with storage lid and freeze for 24 hours. 4. After 24 hours, take off the lid from container and arrange into the outer bowl of Ninja CREAMi. 5. Install the "Creamerizer Paddle" onto the lid of outer bowl. 6. Then rotate the lid clockwise to lock. 7. Press "Power" button to turn on the unit. 8. Then press "SORBET" button. 9. When the program is completed, turn the outer bowl and release it from the machine. 10. Transfer the sorbet into serving bowls and enjoy immediately. 11. Transfer the sorbet into serving bowls and enjoy immediately.

Serving Suggestions: Serve with a topping of pumpkin pie crumbles.
Variation Tip: Use fresh coconut water.
Nutritional Information per Serving: Calories: 137 |Fat: 0.7g|Sat Fat: 0.3g|Carbohydrates: 33.5g|Fiber: 5.1g|Sugar: 23.7g|Protein: 2.2g

Maple Peach Liqueur Sorbet

⏱ **Prep: 10 minutes**   ◈ **Serves: 4**

Ingredients:

2 pounds fresh peaches, peel removed, pitted and cut up
2 tablespoons coconut liqueur
2 teaspoons maple syrup

Preparation:

1. In a high-powered blender, put in peaches, coconut liqueur and maple syrup and process to form a smooth mixture. 2. Transfer the blended mixture into an empty Ninja CREAMi pint container. 3. Cover the container with storage lid and freeze for 24 hours. 4. After 24 hours, take off the lid from container and arrange into the outer bowl of Ninja CREAMi. 5. Install the "Creamerizer Paddle" onto the lid of outer bowl. 6. Then rotate the lid clockwise to lock. 7. Press "Power" button to turn on the unit. 8. Then press "SORBET" button. 9. When the program is completed, turn the outer bowl and release it from the machine. 10. Transfer the sorbet into serving bowls and enjoy immediately.

Serving Suggestions: Serve with a topping of fresh raspberries.
Variation Tip: Make sure to use fresh and ripe peaches.
Nutritional Information per Serving: Calories: 65 |Fat: 0.2g|Sat Fat: 0g|Carbohydrates: 12g|Fiber: 1.2g|Sugar: 11.8g|Protein: 0.7g

Zesty Cherry Sorbet

⏲ **Prep: 10 minutes** ≋ **Serves: 4**

Ingredients:

1 (21-ounce can) cherry pie filling
¼ cup fresh lemon juice
1 teaspoon lemon zest

Preparation:

1. In an empty Ninja CREAMi pint container, put in cherry pie filling, lemon juice and zest and blend to incorporate. 2. Cover the container with storage lid and freeze for 24 hours. 3. After 24 hours, take off the lid from container and arrange into the outer bowl of Ninja CREAMi. 4. Install the "Creamerizer Paddle" onto the lid of outer bowl. 5. Then rotate the lid clockwise to lock. 6. Press "Power" button to turn on the unit. 7. Then press "SORBET" button. 8. When the program is completed, turn the outer bowl and release it from the machine. 9. Transfer the sorbet into serving bowls and enjoy immediately.

Serving Suggestions: Serve with a topping of lemon zest.
Variation Tip: For the best result, use freshly squeezed lemon juice.
Nutritional Information per Serving: Calories: 175 |Fat: 0.2g|Sat Fat: 0.2g|Carbohydrates: 42.1g|Fiber: 1g|Sugar: 0.4g|Protein: 0.7g

Mixed Berries and Orange Sorbet

⏲ **Prep: 10 minutes** ≋ **Serves: 4**

Ingredients:

3 cups frozen mixed berries
½ cup whole milk
2 tablespoons honey
2 tablespoons fresh orange juice
1 teaspoon orange zest

Preparation:

1. In a high-powered blender, put in berries and remaining ingredients and process to form a smooth mixture. 2. Transfer the blended mixture into an empty Ninja CREAMi pint container. 3. Cover the container with storage lid and freeze for 24 hours. 4. After 24 hours, take off the lid from container and arrange into the outer bowl of Ninja CREAMi. 5. Install the "Creamerizer Paddle" onto the lid of outer bowl. 6. Then rotate the lid clockwise to lock. 7. Press "Power" button to turn on the unit. 8. Then press "SORBET" button. 9. When the program is completed, turn the outer bowl and release it from the machine. 10. Transfer the sorbet into serving bowls and enjoy immediately.

Serving Suggestions: Serve with a topping of banana slices.
Variation Tip: Feel free to use berries of your choice.
Nutritional Information per Serving: Calories: 91 |Fat: 1.1g|Sat Fat: 0.5g|Carbohydrates: 19g|Fiber: 3.1g|Sugar: 14.7g|Protein: 1.5g

Quick Orange Beer Sorbet

⏱ **Prep: 10 minutes**   ≋ **Serves: 4**

Ingredients:

¾ cup beer
⅔ cup water
½ cup fresh orange juice
¼ cup white sugar

Preparation:

1. In a high-speed blender, put in beer and remaining ingredients and process to form a smooth mixture. 2. Put it aside for around 5 minutes. 3. Transfer the mixture into an empty Ninja CREAMi pint container. 4. Cover the container with storage lid and freeze for 24 hours. 5. After 24 hours, take off the lid from container and arrange into the outer bowl of Ninja CREAMi. 6. Install the "Creamerizer Paddle" onto the lid of outer bowl. 7. Then rotate the lid clockwise to lock. 8. Press "Power" button to turn on the unit. 9. Then press "SORBET" button. 10. When the program is completed, turn the outer bowl and release it from the machine. 11. Transfer the sorbet into serving bowls and serve immediately.

Serving Suggestions: Serve with a topping of whipped cream.
Variation Tip: make sure to use fresh orange juice.
Nutritional Information per Serving: Calories: 80 |Fat: 0.1g|Sat Fat: 0g|Carbohydrates: 17.3g|Fiber: 0.1g|Sugar: 15.1g|Protein: 0.4g

Tasty Strawberry Ginger Ale Sorbet

⏱ **Prep: 10 minutes**   ≋ **Serves: 4**

Ingredients:

3 cups fresh strawberries
⅓ cup water
⅓ cup brown sugar
¾ cup ginger ale

Preparation:

1. In a high-speed blender, put in strawberries and remaining ingredients and process to form a smooth mixture. 2. Transfer the mixture into an empty Ninja CREAMi pint container. 3. Cover the container with storage lid and freeze for 24 hours. 4. After 24 hours, take off the lid from container and arrange into the outer bowl of Ninja CREAMi. 5. Install the "Creamerizer Paddle" onto the lid of outer bowl. 6. Then rotate the lid clockwise to lock. 7. Press "Power" button to turn on the unit. 8. Then press "SORBET" button. 9. When the program is completed, turn the outer bowl and release it from the machine. 10. Transfer the sorbet into serving bowls and serve immediately.

Serving Suggestions: Serve with a topping of fresh fruit.
Variation Tip: Ginger ale can be replaced with pineapple juice.
Nutritional Information per Serving: Calories: 96 |Fat: 0.3g|Sat Fat: 0g|Carbohydrates: 24.2g|Fiber: 2.2g|Sugar: 21g|Protein: 0.7g

Lemony Plum Sorbet

⏰ **Prep: 10 minutes** 　　 ◆ **Serves: 4**

Ingredients:

1½ cups cola
⅓ cup fresh plums, hulled
⅓ cup sweetened apple juice
¼ cup water
1 tablespoon fresh lemon juice

Preparation:

1. In a high-powered blender, put in cola and remaining ingredients and process to form a smooth mixture. 2. Transfer the blended mixture into an empty Ninja CREAMi pint container. 3. Cover the container with storage lid and freeze for 24 hours. 4. After 24 hours, take off the lid from container and arrange into the outer bowl of Ninja CREAMi. 5. Install the "Creamerizer Paddle" onto the lid of outer bowl. 6. Then rotate the lid clockwise to lock. 7. Press "Power" button to turn on the unit. 8. Then press "SORBET" button. 9. When the program is completed, turn the outer bowl and release it from the machine. 10. Transfer the sorbet into serving bowls and enjoy immediately.

Serving Suggestions: Serve with a garnishing of fresh mint leaves.
Variation Tip: You can use apple cider instead of apple juice.
Nutritional Information per Serving: Calories: 47 |Fat: 0.1g|Sat Fat: 0g|Carbohydrates: 12g|Fiber: 0.1g|Sugar: 11g|Protein: 0.2g

Chapter 6 Gelato

Creamy Raspberry Gelato 58
Sweet Cocoa Gelato 58
Flavorful Coffee Gelato 59
Easy Blueberry Gelato 59
Sugar Hazelnut Gelato 60
Rich Peach Gelato 60
Pistachio and Apricot Gelato 61
Flavorful Marshmallow Chocolate Cookie Gelato 61
Quick Vanilla Honey Gelato 62
Cinnamon Butternut Squash Gelato 62
Healthy Vanilla Pumpkin Gelato 63
Chocolate Nutella Gelato 63
Delicious Cherry Gelato 64
Honey Dark Chocolate Gelato 64
Strawberry and Chocolate Chip Gelato 65
Yummy Acai Berry Chocolate Cookie Gelato 65

Creamy Raspberry Gelato

⏲ **Prep: 10 minutes**   🍳 **Cook: 3 minutes**   🍽 **Serves: 4**

Ingredients:

4 large egg yolks
1 tablespoon maple syrup
5 tablespoons white sugar
1 cup heavy cream
⅓ cup whole milk
1 teaspoon vanilla extract
1 cup frozen raspberries, halved

Preparation:

1. In a small-sized saucepan, put egg yolks, maple syrup and white sugar and whisk to incorporate thoroughly. 2. Add the heavy cream, milk and vanilla extract and whisk to incorporate thoroughly. 3. Place the saucepan on burner at around medium heat and cook for around 2-3 minutes, stirring continuously. 4. Take off the pan of milk mixture from burner and through a fine-mesh strainer, strain the mixture into an empty Ninja CREAMi pint container. 5. Place the container into an ice bath to cool. 6. After cooling, cover the container with the storage lid and freeze for 24 hours. 7. After 24 hours, take off the lid from container and arrange into the outer bowl of Ninja CREAMi. 8. Install the "Creamerizer Paddle" onto the lid of outer bowl. 9. Then rotate the lid clockwise to lock. 10. Press "Power" button to turn on the unit. 11. Then press "GELATO" button. 12. When the program is completed, with a spoon, create a 1½-inch wide hole in the center that reaches the bottom of the pint container. 13. Add the raspberries into the hole and press "MIX-IN" button. 14. When the program is completed, turn the outer bowl and release it from the machine. 15. Transfer the gelato into serving bowls and serve immediately.

Serving Suggestions: Serve with a garnishing of chocolate chips.
Variation Tip: Use the best quality raspberries.
Nutritional Information per Serving: Calories: 256 |Fat: 16.1g|Sat Fat: 3.4g|Carbohydrates: 22.4g|Fiber: 0.4g|Sugar: 19.1g|Protein: 4.1g

Sweet Cocoa Gelato

⏲ **Prep: 10 minutes**   🍳 **Cook: 5 minutes**   🍽 **Serves: 4**

Ingredients:

2 egg yolks
⅓ cup brown sugar
1 cup whole milk
¾ cup heavy cream
1½ tablespoons Dutch processed cocoa powder
1 teaspoon vanilla extract

Preparation:

1. In a small-sized saucepan, put egg yolks and brown sugar and whisk to incorporate thoroughly. 2. Add the milk, heavy cream, cocoa powder and vanilla extract and whisk to incorporate thoroughly. 3. Place the saucepan on burner at around medium heat and cook for around 4-5 minutes, stirring continuously. 4. Take off the pan of milk mixture from burner and blend in the vanilla extract. 5. Through a fine-mesh strainer, strain the mixture into an empty Ninja CREAMi pint container. 6. Place the container into an ice bath to cool. 7. After cooling, cover the container with the storage lid and freeze for 24 hours. 8. After 24 hours, take off the lid from container and arrange into the outer bowl of Ninja CREAMi. 9. Install the "Creamerizer Paddle" onto the lid of outer bowl. 10. Then rotate the lid clockwise to lock. 11. Press "Power" button to turn on the unit. 12. Then press "GELATO" button. 13. When the program is completed, turn the outer bowl and release it from the machine. 14. Transfer the gelato into serving bowls and serve immediately.

Serving Suggestions: Serve with a topping of fresh raspberries.
Variation Tip: Make sure to use Dutch processed cocoa powder.
Nutritional Information per Serving: Calories: 210 |Fat: 12.8g|Sat Fat: 7.2g|Carbohydrates: 22.5g|Fiber: 0.6g|Sugar: 20.4g|Protein: 4g

Flavorful Coffee Gelato

⏱ **Prep: 10 minutes**   🍳 **Cook: 5 minutes**   ≋ **Serves: 4**

Ingredients:

4 egg yolks
⅓ cup honey
1¾ cups whole milk
2 tablespoons coffee powder

Preparation:

1. In a medium-sized saucepan, put in egg yolks and remaining ingredients on burner at around medium heat and cook for around 3-5 minutes, stirring continuously. 2. Through a fine-mesh strainer, strain the mixture into an empty Ninja CREAMi pint container. 3. Place the container into an ice bath to cool. 4. After cooling, cover the container with the storage lid and freeze for 24 hours. 5. After 24 hours, take off the lid from container and arrange into the outer bowl of Ninja CREAMi. 6. Install the "Creamerizer Paddle" onto the lid of outer bowl. 7. Then rotate the lid clockwise to lock. 8. Press "Power" button to turn on the unit. 9. Then press "GELATO" button. 10. When the program is completed, turn the outer bowl and release it from the machine. 11. Transfer the gelato into serving bowls and serve immediately.

Serving Suggestions: Serve with a topping of cocoa powder.
Variation Tip: You can use espresso powder in this recipe.
Nutritional Information per Serving: Calories: 339 |Fat: 26.1g|Sat Fat: 21.2g|Carbohydrates: 23g|Fiber: 0.8g|Sugar: 17.5g|Protein: 5g

Easy Blueberry Gelato

⏱ **Prep: 15 minutes**   🍳 **Cook: 10 minutes**   ≋ **Serves: 4**

Ingredients:

1 cup whole milk
½ cup heavy cream
3 large egg yolks
⅓ cup granulated sugar
1 tablespoon honey
½ cup fresh blueberries

Preparation:

1. In a medium-sized saucepan, put in milk and remaining ingredients except for blueberries pieces on burner at around medium heat. 2. Cook for around 7-10 minutes, whisking constantly. 3. Through a fine-mesh strainer, strain the blended mixture into an empty Ninja CREAMi pint container. 4. Place the container into an ice bath to cool. 5. After cooling, blend in the blueberries pieces. 6. Cover the container with the storage lid and freeze for 24 hours. 7. After 24 hours, take off the lid from container and arrange into the outer bowl of Ninja CREAMi. 8. Install the "Creamerizer Paddle" onto the lid of outer bowl. 9. Then rotate the lid clockwise to lock. 10. Press "Power" button to turn on the unit. 11. Then press "GELATO" button. 12. When the program is completed, turn the outer bowl and release it from the machine. 13. Transfer the gelato into serving bowls and enjoy immediately.

Serving Suggestions: Serve with a topping of chocolate sauce.
Variation Tip: Use fresh and ripe blueberries.
Nutritional Information per Serving: Calories: 219 |Fat: 11.2g|Sat Fat: 6g|Carbohydrates: 27.1g|Fiber: 1.4g|Sugar: 24.9g|Protein: 4.6g

Sugar Hazelnut Gelato

⏱ **Prep: 10 minutes** 🍲 **Cook: 3 minutes** ≋ **Serves: 4**

Ingredients:

4 large egg yolks
5 tablespoons granulated sugar
1 tablespoon honey
1 cup heavy cream
⅓ cup whole milk
½ teaspoon vanilla extract
⅓ cup hazelnuts, chopped

Preparation:

1. In a small-sized saucepan, put in the egg yolks, sugar and honey and whisk to incorporate thoroughly. 2. Put in heavy cream, milk and vanilla extract and whisk to incorporate thoroughly. 3. Place the saucepan on burner at around medium heat and cook for around 2-3 minutes, stirring continuously. 4. Take off the saucepan of milk mixture from burner and through a fine-mesh strainer, strain the blended mixture into an empty Ninja CREAMi pint container. 5. Place the container into an ice bath to cool. 6. After cooling, cover the container with the storage lid and freeze for 24 hours. 7. After 24 hours, take off the lid from container and arrange into the outer bowl of Ninja CREAMi. 8. Install the "Creamerizer Paddle" onto the lid of outer bowl. 9. Then rotate the lid clockwise to lock. 10. Press "Power" button to turn on the unit. 11. Then press "GELATO" button. 12. When the program is completed, with a spoon, create a 1½-inch wide hole in the center that reaches the bottom of the pint container. 13. Put in hazelnuts into the hole and press "MIX-IN" button. 14. When the program is completed, turn the outer bowl and release it from the machine. 15. Transfer the gelato into serving bowls and enjoy immediately.
Serving Suggestions: Serve with a garnishing of extra hazelnuts.
Variation Tip: You can use extract of your choice.
Nutritional Information per Serving: Calories: 269 |Fat: 18g|Sat Fat: 8.1g|Carbohydrates: 22.7g|Fiber: 0.1g|Sugar: 19.2g|Protein: 4.9g

Rich Peach Gelato

⏱ **Prep: 10 minutes** 🍲 **Cook: 8 minutes** ≋ **Serves: 4**

Ingredients:

3 large egg yolks
½ cup plus 2 tablespoons granulated sugar, divided
1 tablespoon maple syrup
½ cup cream cheese
¾ cup whole milk
¼ cup heavy cream
½ teaspoon vanilla extract
1 cup frozen peach chunks

Preparation:

1. In a small-sized saucepan, put in the egg yolks, ½ cup of sugar and maple syrup and whisk to incorporate thoroughly. 2. Put in cream cheese, milk, heavy cream, and vanilla extract and whisk to incorporate thoroughly. 3. Place the saucepan on burner at around medium heat and cook for around 2-3 minutes, stirring continuously. 4. Take off the saucepan of milk mixture from burner and through a fine-mesh strainer, strain the blended mixture into an empty Ninja CREAMi pint container. 5. Place the container into an ice bath to cool. 6. After cooling, cover the container with the storage lid and freeze for 24 hours. 7. Meanwhile, in a small-sized saucepan, put in the peach chunks and remaining sugar on burner at around medium heat. 8. Cook for around 8 minutes, stirring occasionally and mashing to form a thick jam. 9. Take off the saucepan of berry mixture from burner and transfer the jam into a bowl. 10. Refrigerate the jam until using. 11. After 24 hours, take off the lid from container and arrange the container into the outer bowl of Ninja CREAMi. 12. Install the "Creamerizer Paddle" onto the lid of outer bowl. 13. Then rotate the lid clockwise to lock. 14. Press "Power" button to turn on the unit. 15. Then press "GELATO" button. 16. When the program is completed, with a spoon, create a 1½-inch wide hole in the center that reaches the bottom of the pint container. 17. Put in peach jam into the hole and press "MIX-IN" button. 18. When the program is completed, turn the outer bowl and release it from the machine. 19. Transfer the gelato into serving bowls and enjoy immediately.
Serving Suggestions: Serve with a garnishing of fresh mint leaves.
Variation Tip: You can use crème fraiche instead of cream cheese.
Nutritional Information per Serving: Calories: 260 |Fat: 9.7g|Sat Fat: 4.9g|Carbohydrates: 42.3g|Fiber: 2.7g|Sugar: 40.4g|Protein: 4.3g

Pistachio and Apricot Gelato

⏰ Prep: 10 minutes 🍳 Cook: 3 minutes 🍽 Serves: 4

Ingredients:

4 large egg yolks
3 tablespoons granulated sugar
3 tablespoons apricot jam
1 teaspoon vanilla extract
1 cup whole milk
⅓ cup heavy cream
¼ cup mascarpone cheese, softened
¼ cup pistachios, chopped

Preparation:

1. In a small-sized saucepan, put egg yolks, sugar, apricot jam and vanilla extract and whisk to incorporate thoroughly. 2. Add the milk, heavy cream and mascarpone cheese and whisk to incorporate thoroughly. 3. Place the saucepan on burner at around medium heat and cook for around 2-3 minutes, stirring continuously. 4. Take off the saucepan of milk mixture from burner and through a fine-mesh strainer, strain the mixture into an empty Ninja CREAMi pint container. 5. Place the container into an ice bath to cool. 6. After cooling, cover the container with the storage lid and freeze for 24 hours. 7. After 24 hours, take off the lid from container and arrange into the outer bowl of Ninja CREAMi. 8. Install the "Creamerizer Paddle" onto the lid of outer bowl. 9. Then rotate the lid clockwise to lock. 10. Press "Power" button to turn on the unit. 11. Then press "GELATO" button. 12. When the program is completed, with a spoon, create a 1½-inch wide hole in the center that reaches the bottom of the pint container. 13. Add the pistachios into the hole and press "MIX-IN" button. 14. When the program is completed, turn the outer bowl and release it from the machine. 15. Transfer the gelato into serving bowls and serve immediately.

Serving Suggestions: Serve with a topping of pistachios.
Variation Tip: You can sprinkle dried lavender for a unique and fragrant twist.
Nutritional Information per Serving: Calories: 269 |Fat: 15g|Sat Fat: 1.8g|Carbohydrates: 27.3g|Fiber: 0.1g|Sugar: 22.7g|Protein: 5.4g

Flavorful Marshmallow Chocolate Cookie Gelato

⏰ Prep: 10 minutes 🍳 Cook: 6 minutes 🍽 Serves: 4

Ingredients:

1 whole vanilla bean, split in half lengthwise and scraped
4 egg yolks
¾ cup heavy cream
⅓ cup whole milk
2 tablespoons brown sugar
1 tablespoon maple syrup
1 teaspoon vanilla extract
5 tablespoons marshmallow paste
5 chocolate cookies, chopped

Preparation:

1. In a medium-sized saucepan, put vanilla bean on burner at around medium-high heat, and toast for around 2-3 minutes, stirring continuously. 2. Immediately turn the heat at around medium-low and whisk in the egg yolks, heavy cream, milk, sugar, marshmallow paste, maple syrup and vanilla extract. 3. Cook for around 2-3 minutes, stirring continuously. 4. Take off the pan of milk mixture from burner and through a fine-mesh strainer, strain the mixture into an empty Ninja CREAMi pint container. 5. Place the container into an ice bath to cool. 6. After cooling, cover the container with the storage lid and freeze for 24 hours. 7. After 24 hours, take off the lid from container and arrange into the outer bowl of Ninja CREAMi. 8. Install the "Creamerizer Paddle" onto the lid of outer bowl. 9. Then rotate the lid clockwise to lock. 10. Press "Power" button to turn on the unit. 11. Then press "GELATO" button. 12. When the program is completed, with a spoon, create a 1½-inch wide hole in the center that reaches the bottom of the pint container. 13. Add the cookies into the hole and press "MIX-IN" button. 14. When the program is completed, turn the outer bowl and release it from the machine. 15. Transfer the gelato into serving bowls and serve immediately.

Serving Suggestions: Serve with a topping of marshmallows.
Variation Tip: You can use cookies of your choice.
Nutritional Information per Serving: Calories: 347 |Fat: 20.9g|Sat Fat: 4.1g|Carbohydrates: 32.9g|Fiber: 1.5g|Sugar: 21.9g|Protein: 6.6g

Quick Vanilla Honey Gelato

⏰ **Prep: 10 minutes**   📦 **Cook: 3 minutes**   ❖ **Serves: 4**

Ingredients:

4 large egg yolks
½ cup plus 1 tablespoon dark brown sugar
1 tablespoon honey
1 teaspoon vanilla extract
1 cup whole milk
⅓ cup heavy cream

Preparation:

1. In a small-sized saucepan, put in egg yolks, brown sugar, honey and vanilla extract and whisk to incorporate thoroughly. 2. Put in milk and heavy cream and whisk to incorporate thoroughly. 3. Place the saucepan of milk mixture on burner at around medium heat. 4. Cook for around 2-3 minutes, blending all the time. 5. Take off the saucepan of milk mixture from burner and through a fine-mesh strainer, strain the mixture into an empty Ninja CREAMi pint container. 6. Place the container into an ice bath to cool. 7. After cooling, cover the container with the storage lid and freeze for 24 hours. 8. After 24 hours, take off the lid from container and arrange into the outer bowl of Ninja CREAMi. 9. Install the "Creamerizer Paddle" onto the lid of outer bowl. 10. Then rotate the lid clockwise to lock. 11. Press "Power" button to turn on the unit. 12. Then press "GELATO" button. 13. When the program is completed, turn the outer bowl and release it from the machine. 14. Transfer the gelato into serving bowls and serve immediately.

Serving Suggestions: Serve with a sprinkling of pumpkin pie spice.
Variation Tip: You can use full-fat coconut milk instead of whole milk.
Nutritional Information per Serving: Calories: 213 |Fat: 10.2g|Sat Fat: 5.1g|Carbohydrates: 25.9g|Fiber: 0g|Sugar: 25.4g|Protein: 4.9g

Cinnamon Butternut Squash Gelato

⏰ **Prep: 10 minutes**   📦 **Cook: 3 minutes**   ❖ **Serves: 4**

Ingredients:

3 large egg yolks
⅓ cup brown sugar
1 tablespoon honey
1 cup whole milk
½ cup heavy cream
½ cup canned butternut squash puree
1 teaspoon ground cinnamon
1 teaspoon vanilla extract

Preparation:

1. In a small-sized saucepan, put in egg yolks, brown sugar and honey and whisk to incorporate thoroughly. 2. Add the milk, heavy cream, squash puree and cinnamon and whisk to incorporate thoroughly. 3. Place the saucepan on burner at around medium heat. 4. Cook for around 2-3 minutes, blending all the time. 5. Take off the pan of milk mixture from burner and blend in the vanilla extract. 6. Through a fine-mesh strainer, strain the mixture into an empty Ninja CREAMi pint container. 7. Place the container into an ice bath to cool. 8. After cooling, cover the container with the storage lid and freeze for 24 hours. 9. After 24 hours, take off the lid from container and arrange into the outer bowl of Ninja CREAMi. 10. Install the "Creamerizer Paddle" onto the lid of outer bowl. 11. Then rotate the lid clockwise to lock. 12. Press "Power" button to turn on the unit. 13. Then press "GELATO" button. 14. When the program is completed, turn the outer bowl and release it from the machine. 15. Transfer the gelato into serving bowls and serve immediately.

Serving Suggestions: Serve with a topping of sweetened whipped cream.
Variation Tip: Use canned squash puree.
Nutritional Information per Serving: Calories: 203 |Fat: 10.9g|Sat Fat: 5.8g|Carbohydrates: 22.5g|Fiber: 0.7g|Sugar: 19.9g|Protein: 4.5g

Healthy Vanilla Pumpkin Gelato

⏱ **Prep: 10 minutes**   🍲 **Cook: 3 minutes**   ≋ **Serves: 4**

▶ **Ingredients:**

½ cup canned pumpkin puree
4 large egg yolks
¼ cup granulated sugar
¾ teaspoon pumpkin pie spice
1 cup heavy cream
1 teaspoon vanilla extract

▶ **Preparation:**

1. In a small-sized saucepan, put in pumpkin puree, egg yolks, sugar, pumpkin pie spice and whisk to incorporate thoroughly. 2. Add the heavy cream and vanilla extract and whisk to incorporate thoroughly. 3. Place the saucepan on burner at around medium heat. 4. Cook for around 2-3 minutes, blending all the time. 5. Take off the pan of cream mixture from burner and through a fine-mesh strainer, strain the mixture into an empty Ninja CREAMi pint container. 6. Place the container into an ice bath to cool. 7. After cooling, cover the container with the storage lid and freeze for 24 hours. 8. After 24 hours, take off the lid from container and arrange into the outer bowl of Ninja CREAMi. 9. Install the "Creamerizer Paddle" onto the lid of outer bowl. 10. Then rotate the lid clockwise to lock. 11. Press "Power" button to turn on the unit. 12. Then press "GELATO" button. 13. When the program is completed, turn the outer bowl and release it from the machine. 14. Transfer the gelato into serving bowls and serve immediately.

Serving Suggestions: Serve with a sprinkling of cinnamon.
Variation Tip: Pumpkin pie spice can be replaced with warm spices of your choice.
Nutritional Information per Serving: Calories: 219 |Fat: 15.7g|Sat Fat: 8.6g|Carbohydrates: 16.8g|Fiber: 0.9g|Sugar: 13.8g|Protein: 3.7g

Chocolate Nutella Gelato

⏱ **Prep: 10 minutes**   🍲 **Cook: 3 minutes**   ≋ **Serves: 4**

▶ **Ingredients:**

3 large egg yolks
⅓ cup Nutella
¼ cup granulated sugar
2 teaspoons cacao powder
1 tablespoon maple syrup
1 cup whole milk
½ cup heavy cream
1 teaspoon vanilla extract

▶ **Preparation:**

1. In a small-sized saucepan, put in egg yolks, Nutella, sugar, cacao powder and maple syrup and whisk to incorporate thoroughly. 2. Add the milk, heavy cream, and vanilla extract and whisk to incorporate thoroughly. 3. Place the saucepan on burner at around medium heat. 4. Cook for around 2-3 minutes, blending all the time. 5. Take off the pan of milk mixture from burner and through a fine-mesh strainer, strain the mixture into an empty Ninja CREAMi pint container. 6. Place the container into an ice bath to cool. 7. After cooling, cover the container with the storage lid and freeze for 24 hours. 8. After 24 hours, take off the lid from container and arrange into the outer bowl of Ninja CREAMi. 9. Install the "Creamerizer Paddle" onto the lid of outer bowl. 10. Then rotate the lid clockwise to lock. 11. Press "Power" button to turn on the unit. 12. Then press "GELATO" button. 13. When the program is completed, turn the outer bowl and release it from the machine. 14. Transfer the gelato into serving bowls and serve immediately.

Serving Suggestions: Serve in waffle cones.
Variation Tip: Maple syrup can be replaced with honey.
Nutritional Information per Serving: Calories: 327 |Fat: 19.1g|Sat Fat: 8.6g|Carbohydrates: 34g|Fiber: 0.9g|Sugar: 32.9g|Protein: 5.8g

Delicious Cherry Gelato

⏰ Prep: 15 minutes   🍳 Cook: 10 minutes   🍽 Serves: 4

Ingredients:

1 cup whole milk
½ cup heavy cream
3 large egg yolks
⅓ cup granulated sugar
1 tablespoon maple syrup
½ cup fresh cherries, pitted and halved

Preparation:

1. In a medium-sized saucepan, put in milk and remaining ingredients except for cherries on burner at around medium heat. 2. Cook for around 7-10 minutes, whisking constantly. 3. Through a fine-mesh strainer, strain the mixture into an empty Ninja CREAMi pint container. 4. Place the container into an ice bath to cool. 5. After cooling, Blend in the cherry pieces. 6. Cover the container with the storage lid and freeze for 24 hours. 7. After 24 hours, take off the lid from container and arrange into the outer bowl of Ninja CREAMi. 8. Install the "Creamerizer Paddle" onto the lid of outer bowl. 9. Then rotate the lid clockwise to lock. 10. Press "Power" button to turn on the unit. 11. Then press "GELATO" button. 12. When the program is completed, turn the outer bowl and release it from the machine. 13. Transfer the gelato into serving bowls and serve immediately.

Serving Suggestions: Serve with a drizzling of chocolate syrup.
Variation Tip: Use sweet cherries.
Nutritional Information per Serving: Calories: 216 |Fat: 10.9g|Sat Fat: 5.8g|Carbohydrates: 26.4g|Fiber: 0.4g|Sugar: 25.3g|Protein: 4.5g

Honey Dark Chocolate Gelato

⏰ Prep: 10 minutes   🍳 Cook: 10 minutes   🍽 Serves: 4

Ingredients:

¼ cup honey
¾ cup whole milk
½ cup chocolate creamer
2 eggs
3 tablespoons granulated sugar
¼ cup dark chocolate, cut up

Preparation:

1. In a medium-sized saucepan, put in honey over medium-high heat. 2. Cook for around 2-3 minutes. 3. Take off the saucepan from burner and slowly whisk in the milk and creamer. 4. Return the pan over medium-high heat and whisk in the eggs and sugar. 5. Cook for around 4-5 minutes, stirring frequently. 6. Take off the saucepan of milk mixture from burner and through a fine-mesh strainer, strain the mixture into an empty Ninja CREAMi pint container. 7. Place the container into an ice bath to cool. 8. After cooling, cover the container with the storage lid and freeze for 24 hours. 9. After 24 hours, take off the lid from container and arrange into the outer bowl of Ninja CREAMi. 10. Install the "Creamerizer Paddle" onto the lid of outer bowl. 11. Then rotate the lid clockwise to lock. 12. Press "Power" button to turn on the unit. 13. Then press "GELATO" button. 14. When the program is completed, with a spoon, create a 1½-inch wide hole in the center that reaches the bottom of the pint container. 15. Add the cut up chocolate into the hole and press "MIX-IN" button. 16. When the program is completed, turn the outer bowl and release it from the machine. 17. Transfer the gelato into serving bowls and serve immediately.

Serving Suggestions: Serve with a garnishing of chocolate shaving.
Variation Tip: Use semi-sweet chocolate.
Nutritional Information per Serving: Calories: 303 |Fat: 10.5g|Sat Fat: 6g|Carbohydrates: 48.4g|Fiber: 0.4g|Sugar: 44.9g|Protein: 5.1g

Strawberry and Chocolate Chip Gelato

⏱ **Prep: 10 minutes** 🍳 **Cook: 3 minutes** 🍽 **Serves: 4**

Ingredients:

- 4 large egg yolks
- 3 tablespoons granulated sugar
- 3 tablespoons strawberry jam
- 1 teaspoon vanilla extract
- 1 cup whole milk
- ⅓ cup heavy cream
- ¼ cup cream cheese, softened
- ¼ cup chocolate chips

Preparation:

1. In a small-sized saucepan, put in egg yolks, sugar, strawberry jam and vanilla extract and whisk to incorporate thoroughly. 2. Add the milk, heavy cream, and cream cheese and whisk to incorporate thoroughly. 3. Place the saucepan on burner at around medium heat. 4. Cook for around 2-3 minutes, blending all the time. 5. Take off the saucepan of milk mixture from burner and through a fine-mesh strainer, strain the mixture into an empty Ninja CREAMi pint container. 6. Place the container into an ice bath to cool. 7. After cooling, cover the container with the storage lid and freeze for 24 hours. 8. After 24 hours, take off the lid from container and arrange into the outer bowl of Ninja CREAMi. 9. Install the "Creamerizer Paddle" onto the lid of outer bowl. 10. Then rotate the lid clockwise to lock. 11. Press "Power" button to turn on the unit. 12. Then press "GELATO" button. 13. When the program is completed, with a spoon, create a 1½-inch wide hole in the center that reaches the bottom of the pint container. 14. Add the chocolate chips into the hole and press "MIX-IN" button. 15. When the program is completed, turn the outer bowl and release it from the machine. 16. Transfer the gelato into serving bowls and serve immediately.

Serving Suggestions: Serve with a topping of fresh berries.
Variation Tip: You can use jam of your choice.
Nutritional Information per Serving: Calories: 325 |Fat: 18.4g|Sat Fat: 10.4g|Carbohydrates: 33.4g|Fiber: 0.4g|Sugar: 17.9g|Protein: 6.8g

Yummy Acai Berry Chocolate Cookie Gelato

⏱ **Prep: 10 minutes** 🍳 **Cook: 3 minutes** 🍽 **Serves: 4**

Ingredients:

- 4 large egg yolks
- ⅓ cup granulated sugar
- 1 cup whole milk
- 1 teaspoon vanilla extract
- 1 teaspoon acai berry powder
- 4 small chocolate cookies, crumbled

Preparation:

1. In a small-sized saucepan, put in egg yolks and sugar and whisk to incorporate thoroughly. 2. Add milk and vanilla extract and blend to incorporate. 3. Place the saucepan on burner at around medium heat. 4. Cook for around 2-3 minutes, blending all the time. 5. Take off the saucepan of milk mixture from burner and through a fine-mesh strainer, strain the mixture into an empty Ninja CREAMi pint container. 6. Place the container into an ice bath to cool. 7. After cooling, blend in the acai berry powder. 8. Cover the container with the storage lid and freeze for 24 hours. 9. After 24 hours, take off the lid from container and arrange into the outer bowl of Ninja CREAMi. 10. Install the "Creamerizer Paddle" onto the lid of outer bowl. 11. Then rotate the lid clockwise to lock. 12. Press "Power" button to turn on the unit. 13. Then press "GELATO" button. 14. When the program is completed, with a spoon, create a 1½-inch wide hole in the center that reaches the bottom of the pint container. 15. Add the chocolate cookies into the hole and press "MIX-IN" button. 16. When the program is completed, turn the outer bowl and release it from the machine. 17. Transfer the gelato into serving bowls and serve immediately.

Serving Suggestions: Serve with a topping of banana slices.
Variation Tip: Use the best quality acai berry powder.
Nutritional Information per Serving: Calories: 241 |Fat: 10.2g|Sat Fat: 2.8g|Carbohydrates: 32.5g|Fiber: 0g|Sugar: 20.2g|Protein: 5.4g

Conclusion

There you have it. There is no doubt that the Ninja Creami is an appliance you should have in your kitchen.

You will transform all your favorite ingredients into delectable, creamy, and nutritious dessert treats and quench your thirst during sunny days. Don't worry about the sugar and fat contents of the frozen desserts. The Ninja Creami has functionality that enhances the production of low-fat and low-sugar dessert treaties contents.

If you haven't got one, consider purchasing one because it will save you a lot of time. If you already have one, you can now begin trying our recipes. Feel free to get extra creative and make personalized recipes that will match your liking. Don't forget to use the care and maintenance tips highlighted in this guide, and your device will serve you long enough.

Appendix 1 Measurement Conversion Chart

WEIGHT EQUIVALENTS

US STANDARD	METRIC (APPROXIMATE)
1 ounce	28 g
2 ounces	57 g
5 ounces	142 g
10 ounces	284 g
15 ounces	425 g
16 ounces (1 pound)	455 g
1.5 pounds	680 g
2 pounds	907 g

VOLUME EQUIVALENTS (LIQUID)

US STANDARD	US STANDARD (OUNCES)	METRIC (APPROXIMATE)
2 tablespoons	1 fl.oz	30 mL
¼ cup	2 fl.oz	60 mL
½ cup	4 fl.oz	120 mL
1 cup	8 fl.oz	240 mL
1½ cup	12 fl.oz	355 mL
2 cups or 1 pint	16 fl.oz	475 mL
4 cups or 1 quart	32 fl.oz	1 L
1 gallon	128 fl.oz	4 L

TEMPERATURES EQUIVALENTS

FAHRENHEIT(F)	CELSIUS(C) (APPROXIMATE)
225 °F	107 °C
250 °F	120 °C
275 °F	135 °C
300 °F	150 °C
325 °F	160 °C
350 °F	180 °C
375 °F	190 °C
400 °F	205 °C
425 °F	220 °C
450 °F	235 °C
475 °F	245 °C
500 °F	260 °C

VOLUME EQUIVALENTS (DRY)

US STANDARD	METRIC (APPROXIMATE)
⅛ teaspoon	0.5 mL
¼ teaspoon	1 mL
½ teaspoon	2 mL
¾ teaspoon	4 mL
1 teaspoon	5 mL
1 tablespoon	15 mL
¼ cup	59 mL
½ cup	118 mL
¾ cup	177 mL
1 cup	235 mL
2 cups	475 mL
3 cups	700 mL
4 cups	1 L

Appendix 2 Recipes Index

B
Banana Berry Smoothie Bowl 21
Banana Coffee Milkshake 17
Best Lavender Tea Ice Cream 37
Blueberry Graham Crackers Ice Cream 39
Boozy Chocolate Milkshake 15
Boozy Orange Ice Cream 33
Brown Sugar Walnut Ice Cream 41

C
Caramel Protein and Green M&M Ice Cream 43
Cheesy Cherry Ice Cream 40
Cheesy Strawberry Pudding Ice Cream 30
Chia Banana Smoothie Bowl 25
Chocolate Chip Cookie Milkshake 12
Chocolate Nutella Gelato 63
Cinnamon Butternut Squash Gelato 62
Citrus Blueberry Smoothie Bowl 22
Citrus Mango Sorbet 52
Citrus Peach Ice Cream 32
Citrus Pineapple Margarita Sorbet 48
Creamy Banana Ice Cream 29
Creamy Banana Rum Smoothie Bowl 19
Creamy Coffee Ice Cream 33
Creamy Raspberry Gelato 58
Creamy Rum Ice Cream 36
Creamy Strawberry Milkshake 16

D
Delicious Blue Spirulina Ice Cream 35
Delicious Cherry Gelato 64
Delicious Chocolate Banana Smoothie Bowl 24
Delicious Coffee Coconut Milkshake 14

E
Easy Blueberry Gelato 59
Easy Chocolate Banana Pudding Ice Cream 42
Easy Peach Smoothie Bowl 22
Easy Strawberry Milkshake 10
Easy Vanilla Cocoa Ice Cream 37

F
Flavorful Coffee Gelato 59
Flavorful Marshmallow Chocolate Cookie Gelato 61
Fresh Avocado & Spinach Smoothie Bowl 27
Fresh Peach Sorbet 49
Fresh Pineapple Milkshake 17
Fresh Strawberry & Banana Cookies Ice Cream 45

G
Gingered Pumpkin Puree Sorbet 53

H
Healthy Vanilla Pumpkin Gelato 63
Homemade Caramel Chocolate Chips Ice Cream 41
Homemade Chocolate Ice Cream 31
Honey Dark Chocolate Gelato 64
Honey Oats Tofu Smoothie Bowl 20
Honeyed Strawberry-Banana Smoothie Bowl 24

L
Lemony Apple Ice Cream 36
Lemony Pineapple Sherbet Milkshake 09
Lemony Plum Sorbet 56
Light Kiwi Banana Sorbet 52
Limey Honeydew Melon Ice Cream 35
Limey Raspberry Sorbet 51

M
Mango Banana Smoothie Bowl 23
Mango Cinnamon Milkshake with Walnuts 13
Maple Peach Liqueur Sorbet 53
Mixed Berries and Orange Sorbet 54
Mouthwatering Coconut Pineapple Ice Cream 30

N
Nutritious Avocado Banana Smoothie Bowl 20

O
Orange Peach Smoothie Bowl 25
Oreo Chocolate Milkshake 13

P
Papaya and Banana Smoothie Bowl 19
Peanut Butter Chocolate Milkshake 14
Perfect Matcha Pudding Ice Cream 31
Pistachio and Apricot Gelato 61
Pistachio Banana Ice Cream 43
Pistachio Ice Cream 39

Q
Quick Orange Beer Sorbet 55
Quick Raspberry Yogurt Smoothie Bowl 26
Quick Vanilla Honey Gelato 62
Raspberry Cottage Cheese Ice Cream 44

R
Refreshing Strawberry Sorbet 51
Rich Mango Milkshake 10
Rich Peach Gelato 60

S
Simple Banana & Strawberry Yogurt Ice Cream 34
Simple Mango Sorbet 49
Simple Pistachio Ice Cream Milkshake 16
Simple Vanilla Pecan Ice Cream 46
Strawberry and Chocolate Chip Gelato 65
Strawberry-Chocolate Ice Cream 40
Sugar Hazelnut Gelato 60
Super-Easy Orange Sorbet 48
Sweet Blackberry Ice Cream 29
Sweet Cherry Sorbet 50
Sweet Chocolate Chips Ice Cream 44
Sweet Cocoa Gelato 58
Sweet Mango Ice Cream 34
Sweet Potato and Banana Smoothie Bowl 23
Sweet Vanilla Pistachio Milkshake 11

T
Tasty Chocolate Sandwich Cookies Ice Cream 45
Tasty Dragon Fruit & Banana Smoothie Bowl 27
Tasty Peanut Butter Strawberry Milkshake 09
Tasty Strawberry Ginger Ale Sorbet 55
Tropical Mango Pineapple Smoothie Bowl 21
Tropical Yogurt Smoothie Bowl 26

V
Vanilla Avocado Milkshake 11
Vanilla Banana Milkshake 15
Vanilla Blueberry Milkshake 12
Vanilla Mango Ice Cream 32
Vanilla Pudding Almond Ice Cream 46
Vanilla White Chocolate Ice Cream 42

Y
Yummy Acai Berry Chocolate Cookie Gelato 65
Yummy Ginger Beer Blueberry Sorbet 50

Z
Zesty Cherry Sorbet 54

Made in United States
Troutdale, OR
06/08/2024